Sleeping
FEARLESSLY

Gustava Martin

PublishAmerica
Baltimore

© 2004 by Gustava Martin.
All rights reserved. No part of this book may be reproduced, stored in a retrieval system or transmitted in any form or by any means without the prior written permission of the publishers, except by a reviewer who may quote brief passages in a review to be printed in a newspaper, magazine or journal.

First printing

ISBN: 1-4137-4416-8
PUBLISHED BY PUBLISHAMERICA, LLLP
www.publishamerica.com
Baltimore

Printed in the United States of America

Dedicated to:

Every Patricia, Megan, Colin, Michelle, and Michael:
wherever you are, I pray you are sleeping fearlessly.

My family – My wings when I had forgotten how to fly!

LA, the retirement finally paid off!

The Divine Intervention that taught me to conquer rather than just survive.

Acknowledgments:

The "real" Wagger family, whose tragic life provided the story
Joni – My Articulate Artist
Jessica – My Grammatical Genius
JJ Photography

FOREWORD

It hit me hard! I couldn't find one specific reason for becoming so intrigued. Something about this small cable access television station being given the authorization to broadcast this trial in its entirety led me to wondering why she did it. That led me to wondering how she survived all those years that finally ended with her.

To most, she was only known as the "woman who used her eleven-year-old daughter to kill her husband," or the one who "engaged in unusual sexual activity." When I first became involved, I too looked at her in one or both of those manners. I was one of those people who talked and spoke of her that way. The only two descriptive terms we could remember through all the media hype from the day it happened.

For over a year now, I had kept this murder locked inside my mind. It seemed at times to be far in the back, but nonetheless, it was still there. Anticipating the day when I could hear it all! Full details of this "out of the ordinary" life!

Then the trial began! It was long! While others were chatting among friends, she was alone. When she cried, she cried alone. When she spoke, nobody heard and by now, laughter was non-existent.

After hearing much of the testimony, I realized she had the right idea she just pursued it the wrong way. Maybe she should have left him! Maybe she should have just put up with the abuse, after all, she had for nine years and he was only home twice a month. Then again, maybe she should have just pulled the trigger herself.

Everybody has a right to his or her own opinion. But why should anyone put up with such abuse? Not only her, especially the children! How can any parent sit idly by and watch her own flesh and blood suffer at the hands of another?

For no apparent reason, or at least not a legitimate one!

This story has one purpose. To reveal the types of abuse that occur but go unreported all too often. It doesn't just happen in bad homes or large cities. This is proof! Small towns like ours suffer from the beast too! Whether the verdict is right or wrong is not up to me. In the end, the choice is yours. Not that it really matters now. For her, parts of life are over, parts at a stand still, and parts she looks forward to beginning.

Patricia loved Walter! She loved her children! Sometimes Walter was kind! Those were the times she loved him most. A man once so loving and kind! One for whom she gave up her first born child because that child reminded Walter of Patricia's life that he was not a part of. Patricia went that extra mile! In a violent rage, Walter would physically, mentally, verbally and sexually abuse her. He physically, verbally, and mentally abused the children. The people he swore he loved most in life. More than life itself!

Walter loved Patricia and their three children and tolerated the rest of the world. But all too often, the anger toward the others would come unleashed on his family. Maybe that anger was unleashed once too often. On February 27, 1987, that anger reared its ugly head for the last time. That anger was reversed! Did she really fear for her life and her children? Or had she found another life where there was no room for Walter? Was her daughter just the easy way out? Sooner or later, she knew she would get caught! Was she willing to pay that price to stop the pain?

I'm not really sure how I feel about the murder. It has all become so complicated. There was no doubt about the extent of the abuse this family suffered at the hands of Walter. It was a major price to pay for freedom. Not so much from him, but from the constant name-calling, scrutinizing, beatings, and sexual abuse. The children had all either been a part of the anger or witnessed the outbursts toward their mother and siblings. Who's right or who is wrong? You be the judge! When all is said and done, you will see what lies ahead in "Sleeping Fearlessly."

CHAPTER 1

It was a great day! If for no other reason, I was alive! Alive and only a spectator at what would prove to be one of the most publicized trials in Upland County history. Not to mention a trial that would give everyone listening a quick and astonishing lesson in life as we did not know it.

I, like so many others who filled the courtroom, discovered my seat, and waited for the arrival of the judge, jury, attorneys, and of course, the defendant.

The date was June 12, 1988. The State of West Virginia versus Patricia Jane Wagger. The charge was murder in the first degree, stemming from an incident that occurred on February 27, 1987. She, along with other witnesses on hand, swore to tell the truth, the whole truth and nothing but the truth in front of what must have appeared to be thousands of watchful, judging eyes. She looked straight ahead, never allowing her eyes to veer to the left or the right. Not even to look behind her. All twelve members of the Jury and the two alternates were declared present. The fate of this twenty-nine-year-old mother of four now lay in the hands of the Upland County Judicial System.

For the past year, law enforcement had kept a very close profile of her. She had moved to a nearby town in an effort to avoid all the hype surrounding the case. Somehow, I felt she could not escape it no matter where she went.

Patricia had taken a job working in a nursing home. The only job she had ever been permitted to keep. Her first outlet for the past nine years to have a life without restraints and, in general, be a part of society! The one who held her back from being anything other than a wife and mother was now gone. But what she had become or accomplished in the past year did not matter now.

The trial was being held to find her guilty or not guilty in connection with the murder of her husband, Walter Wagger. All testimony, remarks, and

9

statements made in this courtroom would now be directed to the jury, the five men and seven women who sat off to the right as if they were in the batter's box. Each obtaining every thread of evidence and information in their mind. Absorbing it all! Waiting for the day when they would return to the jury room one last time, try to make sense of it all, and at last, agree to pass judgment. These were the chosen few and, in the end, the only ones with an opinion that mattered.

Circuit Court Judge, the Honorable Terrance Kimble, called the case to order.

"The first thing we will do, Ladies and Gentlemen of the Jury, is go to the scene of the incident so you may have a better understanding and clearer picture of how and where the alleged murder took place on February 27, 1987."

Spectators were not permitted to travel to the scene. Only the judge, jury, circuit clerk, attorneys, and Patricia herself, escorted by local law enforcement. Cars were waiting for them outside the courthouse to make the trip, and within forty-five minutes, they were standing in front of the little house, now only referred to as "the crime scene" on Glendon Road, in the southern part of Upland County.

The last time Patricia was here was more than a year ago. To many who had seen it before, it still looked the same. To those who had never seen it, it was just another house. To Patricia it was still the last place she called home, and the last time she was here was the beginning of a nightmare. I had to wonder if she could still hear the arguing, the name-calling! Could she still feel the beatings and experience the sexual abuse? Did she see Walter lying in the chair, hear his groaning from the pain, and see the bullet hole just below his chest? Or did she just see the emptiness and sigh at the thought of it being over? At any rate, it was not the same as it had been on that dreadful day. Only an imaginary version of where the victim was lying upon arrival of law enforcement and emergency service personnel.

Patricia still possessed a clear picture of the night in question. She could hear the sounds of the gun discharging and the pain echoing through the walls of this now empty dwelling. The house that seldom held love between a man and his wife. A house all too often adorned with physical and emotional abuse. A house filled with a mother, a wife and four children who only knew peace when the husband and father went away. Yet, this was the place they called home! For two hours they remained on scene as they listened to the authorities describe, in their own words, the appearance of this house in the early morning hours of February 27, 1987.

I often wondered how the actual picture of this home could be viewed from only one night. But that one night was the only time in which this group of people was interested. I sat in the courtroom during the period of time the others were on the crime scene, gathering my thoughts as other onlookers revealed theirs.

"An eleven-year-old child would not do such a thing had she not been coerced by another. It was all her mother's fault. How could she put her daughter through all of this and tell her she loves her? She should be the one who takes the blame! They should take those kids from her, whether she goes to prison or not."

These were the feelings of the majority who sat, waiting impatiently. Not for the beginning of the trial, but for the end. I wondered how they had drawn such conclusions. I was in the news media, and I had not heard enough proof of anything to make such diabolical statements. Somehow, they must have known more than I did, but in reality, I had to smile. Small town rumors!

The evidence had not yet been brought forth, but many found Patricia Wagger guilty as hell from the very words "Hear ye! Hear ye! All rise!"

On the other hand, there were those who were keeping an open mind. Who wanted to hear it all. Not passing judgment, not having sympathy, not feeling at all.

News media gathered from as far away as one could imagine, informing their audiences of any outbreaks in the case. It was unheard of, not only in Upland County, but in the state of West Virginia as well. It was news! It was airing dirty laundry, and that was what we, the people, wanted to hear.

Patricia would soon be known all across the Mountain State as the "woman who forced her eleven-year-old daughter to kill her husband!" She was now labeled! That label would go with her long after this trial was over and, for the most part, only remembered occasionally. She was not to be thought of as a woman who suffered from the Battered Woman Syndrome, nor the one who had spent years of pure hell with the man who was now dead. She was only remembered for the crime, not the reason. The courtroom now became silent as the prosecution rendered its opening statements.

"Ladies and gentlemen of the jury, you have been asked here to hear testimony in a case of murder. During this trial, you will hear as many testify to the times that Mrs. Wagger approached them and asked them to kill her husband. But the most important part will be when you hear the testimony of an eleven-year-old child who acted upon the request of her mother to kill her stepfather. This is why we are here today!"

"You will listen as we prove that after two days of arguing, Patricia Jane

Wagger did get her daughter Megan to shoot Walter Wagger. You will hear as the daughter testifies she was in bed and asleep! That Mrs. Wagger woke up her daughter, got her out of bed, gave her a .22 caliber rifle, and stood in the kitchen with her hands over her ears, while she sent her daughter in the living room to shoot her husband. Many will testify that Walter Wagger was a good man. He worked for Naval Van Lines and he provided for his family, sending home every other paycheck!"

"On the weekend before the shooting, he came home to find the family jeep wrecked, and the bills had not been paid. He became angry and told his wife to leave. Mrs. Wagger was familiar with the local 911 system, as you will hear, because she had used it many times. She did not live in a remote area so there was no reason for her to be afraid. Walter had threatened to kill his wife many times before, but he hadn't done it. So why was she so afraid this time as she claims in her defense?"

"You will hear testimony proving that Mrs. Wagger did falsify many statements concerning the shooting which she would later change. Much of the testimony will be contradicting, but we intend to prove that Mrs. Wagger did in fact premeditate the murder of her husband Walter Wagger."

These were some pretty staggering and powerful allegations made by Prosecuting Attorney Allen Marks. If they were in fact able to prove all of this, I knew this jury would find her guilty. But how much could they really prove?

Court-appointed Defense Attorney Carl Ray, was next to give the defendant's version of the case and what was in store in proving Patricia's innocence.

"Members of the Jury, we realize this is not going to be an easy job for you in deciding the outcome of this trial. The defendant did have a right to an out-of-county trial, or change of venue, but chose to remain in her hometown and before her own people!"

"The testimony in this case will be sad, emotional, and often shocking. Walter Wagger was a terrorist in his own home. The true victims are the children and his wife. He was an evil man to his family! They were abused more often than not, and when he went on his drinking binges, the abuse was worse. Mrs. Wagger did tell lies during her statements to the officers, but she was afraid. She had used the local 911 system often, but testimony will reveal, how many times the call was ignored. She was even told nothing could be done unless her husband was home when she called. She had left her husband, and he always found her then he would beat her for leaving. Yes, he told her to leave on the weekend before the shooting, but he had taken both sets of car keys. Where was she going to go? How was she to get there? We ask that you consider the fact this woman was abused! That on February 27, 1987, she had taken all she could take from this man."

I thought that, at this point, it was going to be a very difficult battle.

The prosecutor had been re-elected to this office several times by the people of Upland County. For the first time I truly understood why! He had certainly done his homework where this case was concerned.

The defense and prosecution had agreed on one important factor — portions of this case would be devastating. They were right!

Spectators were about to observe and hear of occurrences that, to most of us, did not exist in our little town. These findings alone would make the opinion of Patricia Wagger very much tainted.

My attention was now jolted as Prosecutor Allen Marks called his first witness.

CHAPTER 2

Prosecutor Allen Marks began what would prove to be the beginning of a long ordeal.

There she stood. Not at all what I expected! She looked so fragile! Just a mere child! Knowing what pain was and showing it on her face. Red hair and freckles with a total look of complete innocence.

She knew what it all meant. Why she was here. The fear of losing her mother and yet the legalities of telling the truth. A court system so dependent on the facts, there wasn't time to see the love. I knew this had to be the most difficult time in her young life. Just when she and her mother had finally gotten a chance to be together as a family! What she was about to say today, the truth as to what happened, could end that chance for an eternity.

I knew, just as I was sure she did, it had to be done. Yet I couldn't help but wonder, *Had she not suffered enough?*

With each glance, I wanted to take her and just leave it all behind. Hug her and tell her everything was going to be all right! But how could I possibly begin to make her believe it when I didn't believe it myself?

She had been without her mother, brothers and sister since the shooting had taken place. Living each day with the hope that someday they would be a family again, without the abuse! But today was the beginning of infinity in starting over.

Megan Eursala Billingston, daughter of the defendant and stepdaughter of Walter Wagger, was now twelve years old. She confessed to knowing the difference in telling the truth and telling a lie.

She was born October 22, 1975, out of wedlock to seventeen-year-old Patricia Jane Billingston, who was still a child herself at the time. Until Walter came into the picture, she and her mother grew up together. They were more like sisters than mother and daughter. Sometimes they were all each other had. Had it not been for Patricia's parents, nobody would have cared for this child at all once Patricia became involved with Walter.

She lived with her grandparents, only seeing her mother when Patricia would leave Walter for a short time or on those rare occasions when he was in a good mood and would bring Patricia for a visit.

Then, in October 1986, Walter consented to Megan and her grandmother coming to live with Patricia and her family.

Just by watching Megan, one could tell that she was an adult living in a child's body. As the line of questioning began, she raised her small hand and swore to tell the truth "so help me God." Her first task was to observe the .22 caliber rifle that had been found at the crime scene and was now entered into state's evidence as the murder weapon.

Prosecutor Marks began.

"Megan, is this the weapon you used to shoot Walter Wagger?"

"Yes." Her voice was soft. Hearing her was almost as difficult as finding a seat in the courtroom.

"Can you tell us what took place on the weekend leading up to the shooting?"

"Yes..." She paused as though waiting for a signal to continue.

"Go ahead." Prosecutor Marks gave her that approval.

"This guy from Florida was dating Mom. On Friday, he had asked her if he could borrow the jeep to go pick up some stuff. He kept asking. She finally told him he could borrow it. He wrecked it! When Walter came home on Saturday, he got mad at Mom because she let him borrow the jeep. Then he said she had not told him the jeep had been wrecked."

"Megan, do you know if your Mom talked with Walter the night before he came home?"

"Yes."

"And did she tell him the jeep had been wrecked?"

"Yes. That is why he came home I think."

"Do you know the name of the guy your Mom was dating?"

"Yes. It was Wade Bradsworth."

"Go ahead with that weekend."

"Walter got real mad and he went to the Harald Apartments to see if anyone over there knew what was going on. And I guess he was asking around if Mom was dating Wade Bradsworth."

"Did he ask you or your brother and sister if you knew what had happened to the jeep?"

"No. He didn't talk much to us."

"Megan, do you recall Walter hitting your Mom any on Saturday?"

"No. He wasn't home much on that day."

Megan was constantly allowing her eyes to move into the direction of her mother. She moved her thumbs in a circular motion and invariably moved her hands as though she was somewhat nervous. She displayed a look of terror in this trial, but no remorse toward the incident. She was sincere and very much believable in her testimony. I knew whatever this child said was going to make a big impact on the jury. But so much of what had occurred that weekend still remained unheard.

"Megan, please continue."

"On Sunday Walter got up and started fighting again. He hit Mom a lot that day. I got up early and went to church. Then when I came home, they were still fighting. I fixed the kids and Grandma something to eat. Walter came into the kitchen. I gave him a plate but he threw it in the floor and told Mom to pick it up. She couldn't though cause her arms were too sore from where he had hit her. Grandma was sitting at the table and she told Walter to pick it up himself. Then he called Grandma an old bag and slapped her beside the head. I was standing by the kitchen stove and he pushed me into the wall. He told Mom to pack her clothes and to take me and Grandma and leave. He was gone a lot that day. He went over to the Harald Apartments and was asking again if Mom was dating Wade Bradsworth. Mom asked me two or three times Sunday if I could kill Walter, but I said no!"

"Megan, did you see Walter with a butcher knife at all during the weekend?"

"Yes! He had one at Mom's throat. I don't know what happened though cause he pushed her in the bedroom and shut the door."

"Megan, why do you think your mother wanted you to shoot Walter?"

She hesitated for a moment and flashed a half smile toward her mother as though she was seeking advice. But her mother couldn't help her. Nobody could help her now.

"She didn't want to go to jail, and she thought I wouldn't cause I'm a kid."

Spectators began looking at each other then glancing at the jury in an attempt to see a reaction from one or all of them. However, the seven women and five men showed no expression at all.

"Please continue." Prosecutor Marks stated in a voice seemingly used to convince this child that she was not the criminal.

"When Walter woke up Monday he was madder than ever. All those times he went over to the apartment he never found out anything. He told Mom her friends were just protecting her. He went into town and bought some vodka and orange juice and started drinking. Mom asked me a couple of times Monday if I could shoot Walter and the last time she asked me I said yes."

"Megan, what happened that night after Walter came home?"

"He came home about eleven-thirty and sat down in the rocking chair in the living room. Then he got up and went into the kitchen to fix him another drink. I was fixing me and Michelle, my little sister, some sauerkraut and wieners and he told Mom he wanted something to eat. Then he went back into the living room and sat down. Mom asked me to fix him something to eat because she was still too sore from the beatings. So I did! He came back in, fixed him another drink. The bottle was almost empty now! He went back into the living room and sat back down in the rocking chair. Then he came back into the kitchen and told Mom that he thought he told her to be gone when he got home. He said he was going to kill her if she was still there when he woke up. I was afraid he would. I fixed him some food but when I took it into him he was passed out in the chair."

Her eyes posed an innocent glance toward her mother, but only for a brief moment before the prosecution continued.

"Then what happened?"

"Me and Michelle finished eating and then we went to bed."

"Did you get back up?"

"Yes! Mom came into my bedroom and sat down on the bed. She told me she was going to shoot him but her hands were too shaky. She told me to get up so I did. Me and Mom went into the kitchen. She gave me the gun and told me to go into the living room and shoot Walter. I took the gun, went into the living room, and pulled the trigger, but the gun didn't go off. I went back into the kitchen and Mom was standing there with her hands over her ears. I told her the gun wouldn't go off and she told me to pull harder. I went back into the living room, put the gun next to his chest, and pulled harder, but the gun still didn't go off. I went back into the kitchen and told Mom. She checked the gun, told me she thought shooting him in the stomach would kill him, and told me to try again. So I did and this time I shot him."

Third time is a charm, I thought. *She had three chances to stop this from happening. But she just insisted more.*

For a brief moment, the courtroom was silent. Prosecutor Marks rubbed his chin as though he was in deep thought. Like he was contemplating his next move.

The child stared at her mother, who continued to look down. No smiles or facial expressions were exchanged between the two at that moment. I felt sick to my stomach. I wondered how much worse this could become. Was this the shocking story we had all been waiting for? I knew the defendant had yet to tell her side, but I became nauseated at the mere thought of this child having gone through such torment. How would she ever outgrow these memories!

"Megan, what did you do after you shot Walter?"

"I put the gun under the bar in the kitchen and then I went back to bed. I could hear him groaning in the living room, but I just laid there until the officers arrived."

That seemed like the logical thing to do. She had been awakened for the sole purpose of shooting Walter. Having accomplished this, why stay in the room and see the result? Wasn't it enough having to hear it from a distance?

"Megan, what did you tell the officer when he asked you about shooting Walter?"

"Well me and Mom had talked and she told me to tell him that she was on the couch asleep when I shot Walter, so that is what I told him."

"Megan, would you have shot Walter had your mother not told you to?"

"No!" Megan replied without hesitation but with a sound of doubt. Not doubting her answer or the truth behind it, but more so doubting whether her answer was going to send her mother to prison.

Prosecutor Marks then asked Megan about an interview she; her mother; and her brother, Colin, had given to a local television station reporter later that day after Walter had been shot.

"Megan, what did you tell the news reporter happened on the night Walter was shot?"

"The same thing I told the officer. Just like Mom told me to do! That she was asleep on the couch when I shot Walter. I thought he was going to wake up and kill Mom and so I shot him."

I paused for a moment, as the prosecution had no further questions. I had to contemplate on how much control this woman had over her child, just as Walter had controlled her. I couldn't help but wonder how far Megan would have gone on the mere command of her mother. While Megan showed no remorse toward what she had done, my heart went out to her. Did she fully understand what had taken place, or was she just relieved that the pain of abuse was gone?

At the tender age of twelve, she was personally experiencing what most children her age were forbidden to watch on television.

When I brought myself back to what was taking place in this courtroom, the prosecution and Defense were trading places. Almost like the changing of the guard! This gave everybody an opportunity to breathe and try to remember all they had accumulated from the testimony of just one witness. We would now hear a different segment in the life of Megan Eursala Billingston.

Defense Attorney Carl Ray began!

"Megan, how did Walter treat you?"

"He beat me a lot and always called me a red-headed bitch. He told me that Mom found me under a garbage can and felt sorry for me so she took me home with her. He whipped me and my brother Colin a lot with the belt or a limb, sometimes for no reason."

"Do you ever remember a time when Walter threatened you with a mouse trap?"

"One time when Colin opened a can of potted meat and didn't eat it. Walter came home and saw the can in the garbage. He wanted to know who opened it. Colin said he didn't do it and I said I didn't do it. Walter said he was going to put our fingers in a mousetrap if we didn't tell him who had done it. He brought a mousetrap in and let it go off in front of our face. He kept setting it and letting it go off. Then he said the next time he was going to put our fingers in it so someone better tell him who had done it. So I said I did."

"Did he set off the mouse trap on your fingers?"

"No! He just beat me with his belt."

"Do you remember an incident involving black pepper?"

"One time Colin got a piece of chocolate cake without asking for it. Walter made him lay down in the floor and put his head back, then Walter poured black pepper in his mouth. It got into his eyes and Colin started crying. But Walter said that would teach him to get things without asking."

Her voice began to quiver more as she spoke, and her hands moved faster. I found myself staring intently, but not once did her eyes meet mine. She looked at no one except her mother and the one asking the questions. She bit her upper lip in between answers. Often, she hesitated before answering, but only for a split second. Not long enough to fabricate any portion of her testimony. Her only emotions appeared when she spoke of the abuse toward her mother and brother. I believed she was saying exactly what had happened to the best of her recollection. Just by paying close attention, one could tell she had not been coached. It was clear the incident, which had occurred more than a year ago, was still very much a part of her memory. I was certain what she had lived through could not be easily forgotten. Her memory was clouded only by the sight of her mother, nestled between two lawyers, listening to the terrible things being said about her. Patricia was used to hearing derogatory remarks being made about her, but this time they were coming from the mouths of babes. Her own!

"Megan, why did you kill Walter?"

"Because I was afraid he was going to kill Mom."

"Why didn't your mother shoot him?"

"She said she was afraid she would drop the gun."

"Had you been beaten by Walter any that weekend?"

"Yes! I had bruises on my arms from where Walter hit me."

"Do you know if your Mom ever left Walter?"

"Yes! She came to Grandma's one time, but Walter came and took the other two kids so Mom went back."

I thought how special this little girl was. Her mother had given her up once for this man. Then, when her mother left him and came back, Megan welcomed her with opened arms. Her mother went back to this man because of the two children they shared, leaving Megan behind once again. But this child fought for her mother and these two children right to the bitter end. She was someone special then, and somehow, a part of me knew she always would be!

Megan looked very much relieved when neither the prosecution nor the defense had any further questions. She glanced toward her mother as if she were waiting for a pat on the back. Somebody who would look at her and say, "Good job!"

Even though I could not see the defendant, I could feel the exchange of smiles between she and her daughter. I knew they both shared that special love in their hearts. The love even the court could not remove. A love that even Walter Wagger had not been able to eliminate. It was as though looks were saying much more than words. How that little girl must be feeling! Wondering if her answers, being truthful, would send her mother to prison! Would her mother ever look at her the same after her testimony? I wondered how her brothers and sister were feeling toward her at this moment. Yes, the abuse was gone, thanks to Megan, but so was the family as they knew it.

At the age of twelve, Megan had already grown up in so many ways. She never knew her biological father, and her stepfather hated her. She had spent the better part of her life without her mother and been raised by her grandparents. In 1981, her grandfather died, leaving her to take care of her ailing grandmother alone. After finally moving in with her mother, she watched as Walter abused the entire family. Her mother, her grandmother, her brother, and sister! She listened as he called her names and felt the pain of his anger. At age eleven, she had already served as a teacher, a baby-sitter, and even a mother to the younger children.

She often took on the duties of her mother. Feeding the children, bathing them, changing diapers, and doing the household chores. She even lied, saying she had committed offences, just to keep the younger children from being abused. At age eleven, she was a martyr, sacrificing herself for her family. Now she was on the witness stand telling strangers how she had done it again. This time for her mother. She would stop at nothing to find that freedom she and her family longed for. No matter what sacrifice she made, nothing could make the abuse go away.

Megan attended church and often prayed for a better situation. For a way to make the pain stop.

With one last glance at her mother, she accepted permission to leave the witness stand. She had survived! But how much had she lost in this last attempt to take care of her family?

CHAPTER 3

The prosecution called its next witness.

Deputy Vincent Maracos stood at least a foot above the tallest person in the courtroom. I would have guessed his height to be about seven feet and weight to be close to three hundred pounds. He appeared to be all muscle! I was astonished at the height of this man. Even though I had seen him several times and had even stood next to him in conversation, never had he seemed so heightened. I wondered if either of the two attorneys would dare dispute any of the evidence brought forth by this man. I kept thinking of how frightened any adult would be at his size. How terribly intimidated the Wagger children must have felt when he entered their home! He, without a doubt, was Upland County's version of Paul Bunyan. But, in spite of his size, he wore a kind face and spoke in a soft voice. He was out to hurt no one; he was just doing his job.

Vincent was the primary investigating officer, having been first to arrive on scene, in the murder case of Walter Wagger. With thirteen years of law enforcement experience behind him, he was definitely the man for the job. He began his testimony by stating his name and, without the slightest hesitation, began to explain how he had become involved in the case.

"I was in the vicinity when the call came from Comm Center, our dispatch center. I was told by the dispatcher that Mrs. Wagger called 911 stating she had shot her husband. I responded to the scene, along with Conservation Officer John Vorinski. The time was approximately 12:47 on the morning of February 27, 1987. Upon entering the residence, I located the victim, Walter Wagger, lying on his back on the living room floor. I spoke with Mrs. Wagger who immediately told me she did not know what had happened. That her daughter had shot her husband."

22

A chill ran down my spine! After hearing Megan's testimony, I knew that Patricia did know what happened. I was anxious to hear how she would explain in her testimony the change of heart from the time she called 911 to the time the officers arrived. I kept thinking she must have been scared at the time she placed the call, realizing what had happened, asking herself what she could have done differently, and suddenly realizing nothing! She had no time for second thoughts, especially now that reality had set in. Maybe seeing the officer caused her to relive those moments before the shooting, wondering what, if anything, she could have done to change the end result. Maybe she had told the deputy how she had really wanted it to happen. Maybe she thought the pain would just stop. The physical abuse did end, but in actuality, the emotional trauma was just beginning.

Then I thought, maybe she was now just trying to cover her own ass. Turning on her daughter who had followed her request! Maybe if she told them she had shot Walter, authorities would realize this time the call was serious. But, after hanging up, she realized she had made a mistake and began to change her story.

I felt my emotions riding high! I couldn't help but wonder where it would all end. My mind then drifted back to the testimony of Deputy Maracos.

"I examined Mr. Wagger and talked with him. At this time, he was in a semiconscious state. The victim was wearing a burgundy colored western style outer shirt and a white T-shirt under it. I opened the outer shirt and cut the T-shirt, exposing the entrance wound from the gunshot. I sealed the wound, believing the lung had been punctured and waited for the arrival of paramedics."

"Deputy Maracos, what if anything, did you remove from the scene as evidence in this case?"

"I removed both shirts from the scene, a .22 caliber rifle described as the murder weapon, a box of Winchester .22 caliber shells, one spent shell casing, and two bullet fragments. All these items have been placed into state's evidence."

"What did you do after the paramedics arrived?"

"I traveled with the victim to St. Jacob's Hospital where I remained until Mr. Wagger was taken by helicopter to Minnerstown Medical Center."

Deputy Maracos spoke nervously and moved restlessly in the chair as though he was on the witness stand for the first time. I had to grin at the slightest notion of this man being intimidated by anything. Three times the size of Megan and three times as scared!

"Deputy Maracos, were you able to get any response from the victim during the time you were with him?"

"Somewhat… he kept repeating that he was going to die."

It puzzled me as to why the victim, knowing or at least thinking he was going to die, did not ask for his wife or any of the children. Nor did he ask what had happened to him! Where he was being taken or even who had done this to him. During these last breaths, one would have thought that he would have at least mentioned somebody's name. I wondered how he was feeling at the time, other than in pain. Was he able to think beyond his pain? Did he even know who he was and what had happened to him? After all the abuse his family had suffered at his hands, did he even once think to say, "I'm sorry"? Or did he think that maybe it was judgment day?

These were questions to which I would never know the answers!

A diagram was drawn, as Deputy Maracos continued his description of the crime scene. At this point, the prosecutor completed his line of questioning. It was now in the hands of the defense.

"Deputy Maracos, tell us what Mrs. Wagger said to you when you entered the residence?" Assistant Defense Attorney Lenny Roth began.

"She immediately walked up to me and stated she did not know what had happened. That her daughter Megan had shot her husband!"

"Who all did you see in the house when you walked in?"

"At first there was no one in the living room other than the victim, then Mrs. Wagger came in and later her daughter Megan. Then her son, Colin; Mrs. Wagger's mother; the other two children; and some people I did not know at that time."

"When you cut open the T-shirt that Walter Wagger was wearing, you said you believed the lung had been punctured. What made you think that?"

"I located a small puncture wound to the chest. An entrance but no exit wound!"

"And that is what you based your decision on?"

"Yes, Sir!"

"Deputy Maracos, are you qualified to perform first aid and other types of medical treatment on victims?"

Deputy Maracos laughed. It seemed rather funny to me as well! The thought that this defense attorney, as cocky as he was, would question the credibility of this witness!

"Yes, Sir! I keep my First Aid and CPR cards updated and attend various classes on the two subjects."

"No further questions!"

It must have been a little embarrassing to Attorney Roth, having asked such an offensive question and getting an answer that, in my eyes, made him look more like someone grasping at straws than a lawyer with a purpose. I wasn't quite sure what it was he was attempting to prove, but somehow I felt he had failed.

Prosecutor Marks returned for one last question.

"Deputy Maracos, when did you last hear of Walter Wagger?"

"I got a call at about 9:00 on the morning of February 27, from the doctor at Minnerstown Medical Center who told me that Mr. Wagger had just passed away."

An autopsy was performed on the body of Walter Wagger at approximately 9:30 a.m. on February 27, 1987. Somewhere in the vicinity of nine hours after the shooting had occurred.

CHAPTER 4

I knew that, with each passing witness, the defendant was becoming more nervous. She sat between her lawyers. More so now than ever, I noticed her swiping the hair from around her face. I knew this had to be more than difficult on her, just as I knew the testimony of Megan had been. I kept thinking about what had really happened on that night. We had heard only two witnesses' testimonies: Megan's version of the happenings and Deputy Maracos's account based upon Patricia's statement when he arrived on scene. These two stories did not exactly match! According to Megan, Patricia not only was present and awake through it all, but also had encouraged Megan until the job was done. According to Deputy Maracos, Patricia did not know what had happened! I new the two were conflicting, but my odds were on Megan.

I desperately wanted to get past the prosecution's witnesses and onto the defendant, but I knew that moment was a long time away! Although it was perplexing to understand why, I knew the other witnesses deserved to be heard. The Prosecutor was in no hurry to present the defendant's side of the story. Without further ado, the next witness was on the stand.

Minnerstown Medical Center's Forensic Pathologist was on the witness stand describing what he detected upon examining the body of the now-deceased Walter Wagger.

Dr. Justin Jamison began!

"The twenty-nine-year-old body had sustained bruises on the right forearm, two abrasions inside the right hand, abrasions on the skin of the left third finger, and a small abrasion on the left leg."

"Can you give us a description of the gunshot wound?" Prosecutor Marks asked.

"Yes, Sir! To the right, at the bottom of the chest, near the rib line. The bullet had gone through the abdomen then through the liver. It exited through the liver and went into the body cavity, right along the upper line of the pancreas where it lodged. It is my opinion that Walter Wagger died from no other cause than a single gunshot wound."

The prosecution was quick to conclude the questioning of this witness, and I was anxious to hear the questions brought forth by the defense. One particular question I wanted answered was whether Dr. Jamison had an opinion as to the cause of the bruises and abrasions on the body of the deceased. However, the defense had no questions. *What?*

The emotions were becoming quite confusing now. Sympathy for Megan for being dragged into an abusive life, yet an inkling of sympathy for the abuser suddenly turned victim. The pain he must have been going through at the time just before his unexpected death. The periods of semi-consciousness, when he knew he was going to die. Possibly the feeling of fear — the feeling he had instilled in his family and knew for the first time.

Although I had heard of the abuse from Megan, I still felt murder was not the way out. There must have been other methods of escape! Patricia had asked her daughter to take care of this matter because, for whatever reason, she could not get out of the situation herself. I was beginning to wonder how the defense expected us to find any sympathy in our hearts for Patricia. *Kill the bastard if you must, but why use your daughter to do it for you? When you should be protecting your child, she is the protector.*

I could not recall ever being in such a complex situation. Not knowing which end was up! Who was right or who was wrong. I was saddened by the entire predicament in which he, Walter Wagger, had placed this family. There didn't seem to be much time to dwell on the testimonies at this time because people were on and off the witness stand as though the verdict could not wait. I had to wonder how the jury could consume so much information in one day. Without warning, it was time to continue.

Lawrence Pinkerman, Deputy Sheriff of Upland County, had offered his assistance to Deputy Maracos in the wake of the Wagger murder. He had twelve years of law enforcement experience and had now become involved in this highly publicized case.

At the request of Prosecutor Marks, Deputy Pinkerman began.

"On February 27, 1987, I traveled to Minnerstown Medical Center in reference to an autopsy scheduled to be performed on the body of Walter Wagger. I observed the autopsy and was given a bullet fragment by Dr.

Jamison, who performed the autopsy. I brought the bullet fragment taken from the body of Mr. Wagger back to Upland County Sheriff's Department and gave it to Deputy Maracos."

His testimony was concise. He had little to do with the case, other than autopsy observation and bullet transportation. However, he did confirm that the bullet, entered into evidence, was taken from the body of Walter Wagger. He answered each question directly and without hesitation. Deputy Pinkerman was not a tall man, about 5'9", with reddish hair, average build and a pleasant face. It puzzled me. Television always made the cops look so tough and mean, but all the ones in this county seemed to look more pleasant than the attorneys or average businessmen. So far, Deputy Pinkerman's testimony was the only one that did not require finding guilt or placing blame.

The next witness also had something in common with the three previous witnesses. Captain Charles Langford of the West Virginia Department of Public Safety Criminal Identification Lab had examined the bullet fragment in the Forensic Lab, where he was employed.

"It is my opinion the bullet fragment sent to me which was taken from the body of Walter Wagger was indeed fired from the weapon removed from the murder scene."

How could he possibly know this? I knew I did not understand all of the forensic material, but I could not for the life of me figure out how he possibly could tell this bullet fragment came from the same gun. To no surprise, it was not explained!

"Captain Langford, can you tell us what conclusion you have drawn by the test you performed on the residue?"

"The closer the gun is to the body, the more residue is found on the body. According to my calculation, the distance of the gun from the body of Walter Wagger was approximately one inch or less from the outer shirt when the gun was discharged."

The defense took its time in preparing to ask one question.

"Captain Langford, what did the residue test you performed on Patricia and Megan conclude?"

"There were no residue samples found on Mrs. Wagger, but residue was located on the daughter."

This certainly confirmed what Megan had admitted all along. Who shot Walter was not an issue. The purpose for being here was not to determine who shot him, but rather who was responsible. This is when I realized I was becoming too involved! I was beginning to analyze every little detail. No one else in the courtroom could have questioned the validity of every statement being made any more than I did. I wanted desperately to keep all of this in perspective and remember exactly what I was doing here. This was just a part of my job! I was not to become personally involved, nor was I to find fault in those asking the questions or giving the answers. However, this was now asking the impossible. By now it was entirely too late!

CHAPTER 5

Upland County Deputy Sheriff, Mitchell Knicely, was next on the stand. He had been subpoenaed by the prosecution, just as the others who had taken part in this investigation.

"I traveled to the Wagger residence in the early morning hours following the shooting to act as a backup for Deputy Maracos. I arrived on scene at approximately 1:00 am."

"Deputy Knicely, tell us what you found upon your arrival at the scene and what part you played in the investigation."

"Inside the Wagger home Deputy Maracos was working with the victim. Several people were standing around, including Mrs. Wagger; her daughter, Megan; and Conservation Officer John Vorinski. I began obtaining evidence and taking statements from witnesses in an effort to find out what had taken place. I removed a couple of butcher knives from the scene that were laying on the counter next to the murder weapon. Approximately fifteen minutes after I arrived, I took Mrs. Wagger outside to my cruiser to obtain a statement from her concerning the shooting. I began asking her questions as to what had taken place and who had shot Walter. She seemed more interested in telling me about the beatings she had received from her husband than she was in telling me about the shooting."

"How did Mrs. Wagger appear to you at that time?"

"She was a little upset, but nothing major."

So what determined "a little upset"? My God! The woman's husband was inside, somewhere close to thirty yards away, on the verge of dying! Her emotions were being categorized. A little! Nothing major! And the Defense had no objections!

"What did Mrs. Wagger, in her statement, tell you had happened?"

"She said that her husband came home about eleven thirty, and he was drunk. He passed out in the chair, and she laid down on the couch and fell asleep. Something woke her up, but she didn't know what it was. It was after she woke that she realized her daughter Megan had shot her husband."

"Did Mrs. Wagger read the statement once it was complete?"

"Yes, and she said everything was right. She signed the statement and made no corrections at that time."

I was surprised when Defense Attorney Ray actually stood up to ask a question. I wanted to applaud and welcome him to the trial.

"Deputy Knicely, do you recall ever receiving any calls from the Wagger family or Mrs. Wagger?"

"Yes, several times."

"Do you recall any calls from any of them that weekend?"

"No! Our department receives three or four calls a week from the Harald Apartments. Kids fighting with kids, neighbors fighting with neighbors, and yes, Mrs. Wagger stating that her husband was beating on her and the kids."

"You stated that Mrs. Wagger seemed a little upset, but nothing major. What did you mean?"

Deputy Knicely's face turned a different shade of red as he attempted to answer the question the way Mr. Ray wanted it answered.

"She was nervous, jittery, a little shaky."

"And you noticed no visible signs of injuries on her?"

"No."

It's 1:15 in the morning. You are outside in a cruiser. How observable could the bruises be? Why didn't the defense ask if they offered to take Mrs. Wagger to the hospital for the alleged bruises? If for no other reason than to confirm her story!

"And you recall no phone calls from the Wagger family on the weekend of the shooting?"

"Mrs. Wagger did call once during the weekend that I recall. She said that Walter was out then but that he had been beating on her, and she wanted to know if there was anything she could do about it. I told her there was nothing we could do. She would have to call us when he was actually hitting on her."

As Deputy Knicely was stepping down, I thought of how this reminded me of the story I heard during my childhood about the little boy who cried wolf. He had cried it so often unnecessarily. Then, at the time he needed someone to hear him most, nobody listened. Could the murder have been prevented had this one last cry for help been answered? Or was it just a part of her plot?

I couldn't understand the many cries for help, not just this weekend, but so many times before, when no one responded. The more I listened, the more the pieces began coming together. Physical and emotional abuse had now been discussed. She had left, but he always came and found her, bringing her back to the same torture she had fled. Why did she? How could she? Why would she?

Yet when she called seeking help from local law enforcement, she got none! There must have been a reason on both parts. Something beyond my human understanding! If, in fact, he did abuse her, how could she love him enough to stay with him? If she did, in fact, love him, how could she stand in the kitchen with her hands over her ears and pretend nothing was taking place, knowing her daughter was in the next room preparing to shoot her husband?

What was she thinking? Or had it come to the point where she was thinking nothing at all? As the old saying goes, "You can only beat a dog for so long before it turns on you."

Conservation Officer John Vorinski was about to wrap up this segment of testimony.

"I went to the Wagger residence with Deputy Maracos on the morning of the shooting. I then went to the cruiser with Deputy Knicely as he questioned Mrs. Wagger about the shooting and got her statement. She was trying to get us to notice the bruises on her neck. I was in the front seat and she was in the back, so I couldn't notice anything. Deputy Knicely stepped out of the vehicle for a brief moment, and she asked me if I wanted her to continue with her statement. I told her no. She then told me that she had not shot her husband. That her daughter Megan had, but she guessed she was responsible."

Once again, the defense had no questions! I knew there must be a logical rationalization for the defense asking no questions of so many witnesses. I kept reminding myself that it was just a matter of time before it got its turn and the entire case made a complete turn around. I was well ready when the Judge called the next recess. As far as the investigative portion of this trial was concerned, it had come to a close, at least for the moment. The court was adjourned until 9:00 the next day!

CHAPTER 6

The spectators were becoming quite restless. It seemed as though there was a steady flow of traffic entering and exiting the courtroom. People were waiting in the hallway for someone to leave so they could grab the free seat. The entire scene reminded me of playing musical chairs as a child, only in this, the real world, there was no happy music. Starting out the early morning just as they had that very first day! I had gone home last night and could not sleep, visualizing every witness with my eyes closed, trying to remember every pertinent word each one had said.

To me this was all new! I had worked in the media all my adult life, and once a news story was over, it was laid to rest. But this trial, this situation, this family would live in my mind long after this trial was only a part of the unknown history. It was all so difficult to comprehend! How each had survived the way of life they had come to know! It was routine to so many who had appeared on the witness stand.

Even though I had lost much sleep over this, I too could not wait to get back into that courtroom. On Tuesday morning at 9:00, there they were: the very same faces I had left the night before.

Prosecutor Marks wasted no time in calling the first witness of the day to the stand.

Stacha Monroe had been a friend to Patricia in spite of no approbation from Walter. She began her testimony with no apparent regard to anyone, aside from that indicated by her defiant stare at the prosecutor and the occasional glance at her friend!

"On February 27, 1987, at about 1:00 in the morning, Patricia came to Roger Graves's apartment, just across the street from her home. She said she had

33

shot Walter and asked Roger to go over to the house and see if he was dead. About fifteen minutes after Roger left Patricia and I walked over. I went inside and saw Walter lying on the floor in the living room. He had blood on his shirt! He kept saying to the deputy "Please, don't let me die."

More and more, I realized the testimony of previous witnesses was not uniting. First Walter was telling the deputy, "I'm going to die." Then he was repeating, "Please don't let me die." I knew this was all petty, but a woman's life of freedom was at stake here. At this point however, the prosecution apparently felt no need to elaborate on this discrepancy.

"Ms. Monroe, did you, at any time, see any bruises, cuts, or abrasions on Mrs. Wagger during that weekend or on the morning of the shooting?"

"Patricia had bruises on her chest and arms."

Why was it that Stacha could see these bruises, but officers taking the statement could not? Did Patricia just make these bruises appear and disappear at a moment's notice? I realized the lighting was better in the house when Stacha saw her compared to in the cruiser when the officers saw her, but why didn't the deputies find better lighting, if for no other reason than to confirm or dispute the allegations? By now, I had convinced myself I needed to see a psychiatrist.

I was sitting in this courtroom trying to figure it all out! Trying to find a solution to the problem — something not even those qualified had accomplished. I wanted my mind to come back to me; thankfully, I was saved by the next question!

"Did you see the murder weapon at anytime after the shooting?"

"Yes! Megan showed me the gun while I was at their house. The gun was in the kitchen. When Patricia came over to Roger's apartment, she told me she had shot Walter. Then, later on that day, I was talking to Megan, and she said she had shot Walter. She said she hoped the motherfucker died. I was really confused!"

Stacha wasn't the only one confused! Now everyone in the courtroom was looking for answers. Answers that could come only from the defendant! I wondered how, if the defense had done its homework, it had not posed such questions as these to Megan. I wondered if we would ever really know the truth. Did the truth really matter? For the most part, the majority had already drawn their own conclusions and most were not going to change. In fact, most had made up their minds by the time the Judge entered the courtroom more than a week ago. Did it really matter what we heard from this point? The truth was being presented right before us, and we were only listening to what we wanted to hear — selective hearing! We were hearing only what fit our preconceived profile, and that was all we were going to believe.

I was convinced Megan had shot Walter. I was convinced Patricia had encouraged her. The problem lay in the difference between forced and coerced!

Had Patricia forced her daughter to kill her husband, or had she merely given her permission?

The prosecution was finished with Stacha until the rebuttal witnesses would be called. The Defense had no questions! Stacha was not permitted to remain in the courtroom. I noticed as she gave a quick wink to the defendant, her friend, and I could not help but feel her loss. How much would their friendship suffer because of this ordeal? Maybe Walter, in many ways, was still in control of Patricia's life.

CHAPTER 7

Job Thomas was next to be brought forth and sworn in. As a paramedic for the Upland County Emergency Squad, he was in charge of the victim, Walter Wagger, in the early morning hours of February 27, 1987. Job reiterated portions of the testimony presented by Deputy Maracos, and then he began his testimony, describing what he found when he arrived on scene.

"The victim was lying on the floor in the living room of the house. He had a small hole on the right side just below the chest bone. I was unable to get a pulse or blood pressure at that time. I then administered the mast trousers used to help control internal bleeding by air pressure. We then transported Mr. Wagger from the scene to St. Jacob's Hospital for treatment."

Prosecutor Marks barely gave Defense Attorney Ray a chance to say "no questions" before he called his next witness.

Dr. Kevin Ernhardt was working at St. Jacob's Emergency Room when Walter Wagger arrived by ambulance.

"Mr. Wagger arrived at the hospital at 1:45 on the morning of February 27, 1987. He was semi-responsive at the time but had a low blood pressure. We administered a chest tube, and the victim responded to the pain. The only conversation I had with him was when he said, 'Let me die.'"

Here we went again! By now, I figured the pain was so great that Walter Wagger probably did want to die. Just to end the pain. Just as his wife and stepdaughter wanted to end their pain. Subconsciously, he must have known what hell he had put his family through all those years. Its not that he wanted to die; he wanted the pain to die. Those words running through my mind sounded terribly familiar.

"Dr. Ernhardt, what other, if any, medical treatment did you administer to the victim?"

"We rendered a nasal/trachea tube to assist him in breathing. I then notified Dr. Ian Fisher who requested the patient be sent to Minnerstown Medical Center. Approximately forty minutes later, Mr. Wagger was taken by helicopter to Minnerstown Medical Center for further treatment. The next day I did a follow-up on Mr. Wagger by placing a call to the Medical Center. At that time I was told Mr. Wagger had died!"

Once again, Defense Attorney Ray made another surprise statement!

"No questions, Your Honor!"

What the hell were they waiting for? I could not understand why all these witnesses had stepped down with no questions from the defense. Attorneys Ray and Roth could at least have attempted to look interested. This was the doctor who had treated Walter Wagger at the hospital. What about the bruises the pathologist had seen? It might have been nice to know if this doctor had seen any of those. These two lawyers were hired to protect this woman from a lifetime jail sentence and they had "no questions." The last three witnesses had gone on the stand and stepped down without so much as a thank you from the defense. For a moment, I thought I was the one defending this woman. However, in all actuality, I could not think of one question to ask any of the witnesses. None that the prosecution did not ask! What was I looking for? Here was a woman my age, and, while I wasn't everything I wanted to be, I would not have traded places with her for anything in the world. At least I wasn't looking at a possible life sentence in prison.

While I was beginning to mellow out toward the mother, I still had many mixed emotions that kept driving at me. Wanting very much to get to the defendant's testimony and find closure, the wait seemed like an eternity!

CHAPTER 8

Until this point, all of the witnesses, with the exception of two, had been professionals. I knew that, sooner or later, the personal opinions would filter out. Opinions that I knew would wipe away the innocent look on the defendant's face. At the same time, I knew those opinions would affirm the child's testimony of abuse. I contemplated where this affirmation would end. Would we know better, or, at the very least, understand why this occurred in the manner in which it occurred? After the lunch recess, the trial continued with Darlene Trainum. Darlene defined her relationship with Patricia as real friendship. As she took the stand, I noticed Darlene could not look at her real friend. She had to tell the truth even if that meant bringing out impurities both would prefer kept between the two of them.

"I was someone she could talk to! I'd listen! Sometimes we acted like junior high girls, just waiting for Walter's next trip out of town so we could get together. We waited until he went out of town so Patricia didn't have to suffer the consequences.

"I was living at the Harald Apartments in number four when the shooting took place. I had known Patricia and Walter for quite some time. I considered Patricia my friend, but Walter never seemed to like me. Patricia had told me that Walter beat her, but to tell you the truth, I never seen no evidence that weekend. But I really hadn't seen her much cause when Walter is home she don't go nowhere. I had never seen a lot of difficulties between Patricia and Walter, but most of the time when I saw her, Walter wasn't around. I had seen Patricia with men in her vehicle and saw her at parties. She drank on occasion but was never really with no one."

All of her responses were in answer to the questions posed by the prosecution.

She was probably the one person who could discredit the defendant, and Darlene was trying her damnedest not to get caught up in the shrewdness of Prosecutor Marks.

"Darlene, can you tell us what you know about that night and early morning hours after the shooting."

"Patricia came over to my apartment. She was hysterical! She said she had shot Walter. She had meant to kill him, and she hoped to God that he died. She stayed at my apartment. Phone calls from Minnerstown went to apartment five, Harold Carder's apartment. I didn't have a phone. Each time a call came in, Patricia would not go to the phone. Calls came about three or four times wanting someone to come up and sign a paper so they could do surgery on Walter. The last time a call came they said Walter had died."

How did the Minnerstown Medical Center personnel know where to call? It seemed like a logical question to me! The Wagger family had a telephone — that had been proven. There was never any mention as to where the children were while Patricia was over at the apartments giving her version of the event. My guess was that the first time the hospital called the Wagger home, they were told where to call. Logical guess! Maybe speculation! But for now, that was all I had to go on to draw a conclusion. I continuously had to remind myself that this was not a question-answer type situation for speculators. I felt so helpless, so unimportant, so confused! But my life was not on the line!

Hark! The defense attorney spoke!

"What happened after the last call came in?"

"Patricia ran out of my apartment screaming. She began beating on a trailer that was parked outside the apartments. Then she threw herself on the ground and started saying 'I love him. I don't know what I'm going to do without him.'"

There was that word again! LOVE! *Without him, maybe you and your family will have a chance! Maybe this way you can live a little longer!* Thank God, I was too confused to let my thoughts go any further than my brain. Where was my sympathy for the twenty-nine-year-old man who had the life sucked out of him? All of a sudden, it was gone!

During my wide-eyed sleepless nights, I pondered why, during his final stage of semi-consciousness, lasting somewhere around nine hours, he never once asked for or mentioned his family. Never asked to speak with any of them! Never asked who shot him! Why didn't he even take enough time to whisper those words "I love you" or ask someone to tell them for him? Not even his children! Had he ever used those words with meaning? Were those words even in his vocabulary? Maybe he couldn't feel love for anyone! Maybe love was the last thing on his mind, along with making peace with the ones he had hurt for so many years. Knowing that hurt you caused is why you were in this state now. In those final moments of his life and all he thought about was dying.

Darlene was continuing as Prosecutor Marks chose to redirect. Darlene was not a high-society businesswoman by any means. Her dark hair was cropped off and her makeup left much to be desired. Her jeans and knit top were tight and fit snugly around her slender body. With height and weight to fit, she had the makings of a model, but neither she nor anyone else had ever taken the time to explore the possibilities.

"Why didn't Mrs. Wagger go to Minnerstown when the doctor called?"

"Nobody would take her."

"Did you have the opportunity to talk to Patricia later that morning?"

"Yes! I was shocked because, at that time, she told me she did not shoot Walter. Megan did! It wasn't the same story she had told me earlier that morning when she came over to my apartment. Megan was over at my apartment too, but I never noticed any interaction between her and Patricia, but then again I never paid no attention. It was real crazy, you know?"

"Did you ever observe Mrs. Wagger drinking and flirting with men around the Harald Apartments?" Prosecutor Marks continued.

"Yes! But she never got drunk that I remember! She would drink a beer or two, but that was all."

The defense then took a stab, as though they were attempting to make some point of normalcy in the drinking issue.

"Darlene, was drinking a way of life at the Harald Apartments?"

"Yes!"

I knew the answer to that question even before Darlene had answered. From the very first moment I stepped foot in Upland County, I was warned about this area: "Nice girls don't hang out there." But all of a sudden, the very people who had warned me about the area were justifying Walter Wagger having moved his family there. "It was all he could afford," they would say. *Yeah right! And I was born yesterday!*

It was necessary for Prosecutor Marks to have the last word.

"Darlene, did anyone offer to take Mrs. Wagger to Minnerstown that morning when the hospital was calling?"

"Yes, but she didn't accept."

Darlene stepped down from the witness stand looking more bewildered than relieved! I knew she was glad it was over but, at the same time, wondered how much damage she had caused.

It was almost humorous! Had it not been for a life at stake, I might have been forced to laugh out loud. The defense attorney and prosecuting attorney seemed to be playing tic-tac-toe. The one who got three in a row would win, and from where I was sitting, the prosecution was leading by two.

CHAPTER 9

The testimony of Megan seemed a century behind us. It had been so difficult pinpointing the real "victim" in this case. We had heard different versions of the night in question, and while many statements were controversial and conflicting to say the least, my deepest sympathy still went to the daughter. I had to ask, *Just how much guilt did she really have to feel?* Her life with Walter had been a shambles! She had suffered so much from this man, all because her mother "loved him."

Having heard so few witnesses with so many yet to be heard, the trial of Patricia Jane Wagger continued!

"Danielle Thomas, secretary for Attorney Milton Hiller!" she spoke, when asked by Prosecutor Marks to state her name and occupation.

"When did you first meet Walter Wagger?"

"The first meeting took place in 1985, when Mr. Wagger came into Mr. Hiller's office to file for divorce from his wife, Patricia. He stated that on October 21, his wife had gone to Wheeler County with David Vincent and had abandoned their children. He was asking for custody of the two Wagger children and his step-daughter."

"Did he follow through with those proceedings?"

"Not to my knowledge."

"Ms. Thomas, did you have an occasion to speak with Mr. Wagger again?"

"Yes. On February 25th, 1987, he called the office. Mr. Hiller was not in at that time, so I asked if I could take a message. The phone call lasted about ten minutes. He told me he wanted again to file for divorce! He was asking for custody of his now three children and the step-daughter."

"Ms. Thomas, how would you describe Mr. Wagger's demeanor during that conversation?"

"He was very polite, although he seemed a little upset."

"Did he give you a reason for wanting a divorce?"

"He stated that his wife had let her boyfriend drive the jeep and he had wrecked it."

"Anything else he was asking for in the divorce?"

"Yes, the jeep and the motorcycle, in addition to child support and alimony from his wife. He also asked if he could get a restraining order to keep his wife away from him and the children until the divorce became final!"

WOW! I found her statement to be quite powerful! Oh sure, I knew it was probably a part of his plot and maybe just a scare tactic for Patricia! You know the kind that say, "I'll show you! I'll take these kids, get a retraining order to keep you from them, and you will pay me for the freedom to live as you wish." Maybe it was just a threat, but somehow I knew Walter Wagger realized it would work on his wife. Maybe she had not proven to be the best mother, and yes, every day that she remained in that environment, she put her children at risk. But for her to leave without them? I couldn't see that happening!

Defense Attorney Ray asked only one question of this witness.

"Ms. Thomas, what children did you say Mr. Wagger had asked for this time?"

"I believe it was only the three children: Colin, Michelle, and Michael."

Retracted her statement having said he asked for all four.

Where did Megan fit into all of this? She had been separated from her mother for the better part of her life, and now, after cross-examination, we conclude that her stepfather wanted rid of them both. Or so he said! Did Walter hate Megan so much that he did not give a damn about her welfare? Did he love his wife so much that he would hurt and use the children to keep her? Or did he just not like to lose?

Danielle stated that her encounters with Walter were pleasant.

"He was polite," she had said.

We were not only hearing negativity toward Patricia, but the praise of Walter was continuing.

Just when I thought I was beginning to put things into perspective, another testimony reared its ugly head and blew my analysis right out of the water. There was no doubt in my mind that Patricia played the game when Walter was away. But I also knew she lived in fear, not only when he was home, but also that someone would let it slip that she played the game, and he would find out!

I was certain that no testimony would change the fact that this was not my definition of an ordinary family. Not an ordinary home! Certainly not a "brag about" love affair! I thought of how so many people stay in relationships because even bad love is better than being alone. But I had to ask, *Is it really worth it in the long run?* Through it all, I still could not find the root of the bad love.

According to Megan, Walter was an unkind man, to say the least; on the other hand, Patricia was not the perfect wife by a long shot. She dated other men, or at least that's how Megan saw it. She took advantage of a life while he was away and she suffered for it when he came home.

I didn't know where it all began, but, sitting in this courtroom, I sure as hell knew where it all ended.

What lay ahead was a different side of what others saw in Walter Wagger, at least once the defense began.

Prosecutor Marks called his next witness.

Charlene Martin began her testimony with nothing but kind words for her ex-husband, Walter Wagger.

"There was never any physical abuse during our marriage! He was a good father and a good husband. We were divorced in 1979. Walter told me Patricia was pregnant with his baby, and he wanted to do the right thing."

Not only I, but also many others in the courtroom, snickered! Not to make fun of the witness, but did she not know at the time that he was using the pregnancy as an excuse? Such a wonderful man — he was having an affair, had gotten the woman pregnant, and his ex-wife was defending his honor by saying, "it was the right thing to do."

The sad thing was, after all these years, she still did not know the difference!

"After the divorce, he maintained a relationship with our two sons, but I never talked much with him. The last time I talked with him was on February 25th. He called and asked me if I could take care of his children for a while. He told me Patricia had left, and he had to get back to work. He didn't want to lose his job. But I told him no, I couldn't keep the kids, so he hung up!"

"Mrs. Martin, when did you next hear from Walter?"

"I never talked to him no more. The next time I heard anything was when this woman, I don't know who she was, called and told me Walter was dead."

I had to hand it to her. She was determined not to trash the name of her ex-husband, maybe just not to speak ill of the dead. It struck me as odd that Walter beat Patricia and threatened to take the kids, divorce her, and even kill her for having an affair. He was justified by many because of "the way she acted." However, he had done to his first wife exactly what he accused Patricia of doing to him. But Patricia was the only one at fault — he was a saint! What a hypocritical life these people lived! As long as they were not on the receiving end, it was justified!

I immediately saw the sparkle in Assistant Defense Attorney Lenny Roth's eyes. A sparkle that said his next appearance in front of this court was going to bring out a side of the former Mrs. Walter Wagger that she was not prepared to show.

"Mrs. Martin, what kind of husband and father did you say Walter was?"

She glared at him with a blank look on her face, as though suggesting that he not ask her that question again. She had already answered and remembering her initial answer might be a chore. After a brief delay, she replied.

"Pretty good!"

"Did you love Walter?"

"Yes, I did!"

"Then why did you get a divorce?"

Her face was now as red as her hair, and she hesitated before answering.

"Because of her! I would still be happily married if she had not initiated the affair with Walter. It wasn't him! He loved me! But he was also like any other man — a little bit of temptation and they lose their head!"

That was a rather humorous way of putting it! I knew that by raising her voice and becoming redder by the minute, Mrs. Martin was only bringing pleasure to this ever-so-cocky defense attorney. He had not taken a stand up to this point — of course, the defense had not taken much of a stand at all — but he had certainly been the first to bring down the house. It was plain to see that, for Mr. Roth, having this witness, this opportunity, and this kind of attention was sheer ecstasy.

"Mrs. Martin, didn't you file a complaint against Walter Wagger for not paying child support?"

She looked as stunned as a deer with headlights shining into its eyes! If only she had asked — I could have told her no dirty laundry goes unaired when one gets involved in a court of law.

"No," she snapped.

"I have here in my possession a complaint signed by you, or at least it is your name, filed in Greenberg County against Walter for failure to make child support payments."

"Well I might have signed the papers, but I never swore out no warrant."

"And isn't there a signed, certified document filed in the Greenberg County Magistrate's office stating that, quote: 'Walter threatened to beat the holy hell out of me if I didn't give him money'?"

"Yes!"

"But he was a good husband and a good father? No further questions!"

Defense Attorney Roth came in with a bang and went out having discredited the prosecution's witness to unbelief. Well, well, well! Good ole Walter! But now my question was whether Patricia knew what he was before she became involved with him. Of course she did! He was a married man when they began their affair. Only somehow, I believed he convinced Patricia that his affair was Charlene's fault, just as Charlene had believed it was Patricia's. Maybe Patricia just thought she was the one who could change him. Didn't anyone ever tell her that his kind does not change? Maybe someone did, but she refused to listen. She wanted Walter, and not even her daughter could keep Patricia from him.

Damn, this man must have been good! His ex-wife spoke as if she still wanted to be married to him, even though he left her with two children for another woman! To Charlene, he was a saint "because it was the right thing to do." He sacrificed his family because it was the right thing to do! Did he have some kind of overpowering, brain-shaking quality that made these women melt into his arms at his mere command, forgetting all the threats and beatings? But it wasn't his fault. Then whose fault was it?

Walter blamed Charlene when he abused her. Charlene blamed Patricia for her affair with Walter. Walter blamed Patricia for the beatings of her and the children. Yes, good ole Walter was faultless!

So who's fault was it that Walter was dead? Was it Patricia's, because she was responsible? Should we blame it on the abuse? Or on Walter for causing the abuse?

The next witness would prove to be nothing more than a fill-in! Assistant Prosecutor Alvin Smith began his line of questioning with Harold Carder. From previous testimonies, we already knew how Mr. Carder fit into this picture. The calls from Minnerstown Medical Center seeking the whereabouts of Mrs. Wagger came to his apartment.

"Mr. Carder, did you know the Wagger family?"

"Not real good. Wade Bradsworth came to Barberton from Florida with my daughter, and on occasion we would have a party at my apartment and Patricia would come over. I only saw her husband a couple of times around the house. I never saw Patricia exactly with Wade. Only at the party."

"Mr. Carder, do you remember Patricia being at your apartment on the morning of the shooting?"

"No. I heard people talking and the phone ringing, but I had to get up early for work and I just stayed in bed."

Mr. Carder was a man in his fifties, or so he looked. His hair was graying and his wrinkles managed to hide the face of a once good-looking man.

"Did you ever see Patricia Wagger with any cuts, bruises, or abrasions?"

"No."

"Did you ever see Mrs. Wagger with no clothes on?"

At first, I thought the prosecution was trying to imply that Patricia had an affair with this man, too. I could not imagine that! She seemed to lean toward the younger ones!

"Yes, Sir! I saw her go out of an apartment about 1:00 one morning, onto the balcony. She ran down the balcony, down the stairs, then back with no clothes on."

While Mr. Smith was permitting Mr. Carder to face the defense, I thought about the excellent eyesight of this man. He was not only able to tell that Mrs. Wagger had no clothes on, but able to give a clear description of her route of travel. Either his eyesight was better than perfect or the lighting at the Harald Apartments was top of the line. Perhaps Mr. Carder was just more interested in what he was watching than he let on.

Defense Attorney Roth wasted no time in getting to Mr. Carder.

"Mr. Carder, on the night you saw Mrs. Wagger with no clothes on, what exactly happened?"

"Her and Darlene came to my apartment and knocked on the door. Neither of them was wearing any clothes. A bet was made, and they ran down the balcony with no clothes on."

"Was there anyone else up at that time of morning that you know of?"

"No, Sir! I didn't see anyone else."

"Mr. Carder, you really don't know much about this case do you?"

"Not at all!"

"And you really don't understand why you are here today, do you?"

"No, Sir! I have no idea!"

For the first time since the trial began, I felt the defense had finally gotten the final word. I had yet to figure out the validity of Mr. Carder's testimony. The reason for this trial was not to prove how many people had seen Patricia with no clothes on, or how many men she had actually slept with. But deep down I knew that the more the prosecution discredited Patricia, the more they could prove her cause for wanting Walter dead. In bringing out all her adulterations, she, rather than Walter, would look like the bad guy. No sympathy for her would make more of an impact on the Jury when it came time to hand down the verdict. Guilty or not guilty — but of what?

We had just heard two witnesses who claimed Walter was not a bad man, and the next two would prove the same!

Albert Wagger, younger brother of Walter, would admit to having visited his brother's home on rare occasions.

"Mr. Wagger, did you ever observe any problems between Walter and Patricia or ever see any cuts, bruises, or abrasions on her?"

"No."

His testimony was short and to the point.

"Mr. Wagger, when was the last time you spoke with your brother, Walter?"

"I received a call from Walter on February 24. He told me about the jeep being wrecked. He said his wife was running around on him! He wanted to know if I could keep the kids until he could find them a place to live in Virginia. I told him we just couldn't."

Now this was brotherly love! Everybody loved Walter — he was a good man — but in his time of desperation, all of the people who loved him had an excuse for not helping him. Was it him they couldn't help? Or was it his kids? I felt Albert and Charlene were just in this to relieve the guilt. Walter was dead now, so they didn't want to make him look any worse than necessary. But then I remembered they were family, and sometimes families just stand beside each other. No matter what.

On Monday, Walter had gone into town, allegedly to take care of some unpaid bills. He went to Benton's Tire Service Center to get a tire for the car. Tom Benton took the stand to explain his visit from Walter.

"He came into the shop to get a tire fixed. He asked me if his wife had paid anything on the bill. I told him no, and he said he would send me some money. He had always paid his bill! He seemed really upset that this had not been paid. In all my dealings with Mr. Wagger, I never saw him as a violent and quarrelsome man."

Defense Attorney Ray took this one with only one question.

"Did you ever send Mrs. Wagger a bill for the money owed you?"

"No."

Boom! We were just thrown another curve ball. Mr. Benton was a well-adjusted businessman in a neighboring county. His business had survived the difficult times when many others were going under, and it was a family business that dated back generations. To hear him speak highly of Walter, the phrase "not a violent and quarrelsome man" seemed to bear a different meaning. The mixed emotions were there again!

I was looking at the defendant the same way I had in the beginning. If Walter was that abusive at home, how could so many people have such a high opinion of him? What did he do? Just turn the abuse on and off when he desired? Or did the abuse only occur when he was drinking? Why was it that the abuse only happened when he was with his family, the ones he claimed to love most?

I had to remind myself once again that these witnesses were subpoenaed by the prosecution, and they were not going to degrade this man. They were only being asked questions that required answers praising Walter. I was not to hear anything kind about Patricia at this point in the trial, nor was I to hear any reason that would fault Walter for the shooting. The jury was to find Mrs. Wagger an unfit mother and a cheating wife. Walter was to be seen as the perfect husband and father, putting the welfare of his family first. But was he getting in the way of his wife's new freedom? This ploy by the prosecution seemed to be working!

CHAPTER 10

We had sat and listened as many told what a kind man Walter Wagger had been. These people had never seen him violent or quarrelsome. Two of them had known him for the majority of his life. How much longer would we have to wait to hear Patricia's good points? Her life with and without Walter. The before, the during, and now the after!

Apparently, long enough to hear others discredit her character and do it happily!

Eighteen-year-old Chad Miller lived at the Harald Apartments during the time the family lived across the street. But then again, for the most part, hadn't all of the witnesses?

Prosecutor Marks took this opportunity to reveal the partying that Patricia had taken part in while Walter was away, according to the gospel of Chad Miller.

"Yes, I had seen Patricia at parties almost every night. She drank alcohol just like everyone else! Many times, she stayed until 2:00 or 3:00 in the morning. She was always playing around with me!"

"What do you mean by playing around?"

"She was always putting her hand on my leg, stuff like that! I thought she wanted to go to bed with me!"

Almost another laugh out loud point! Was this an over-confident boy or what?

"Mr. Miller, did you see Walter Wagger on the night of the shooting?"

"Yes. He came over to my apartment at about 9:30 and asked me who was driving the jeep when it was wrecked and who his wife was messing around with while he was gone. I told him I didn't know the answer to either question. Then I saw him again about 11:00 or so. He was on the balcony, highly intoxicated! I saw him go into his house and sit down in the chair. That was the last time I saw him, cause I went back inside. I figured there was going to be a fight, and I didn't want to be a part of it."

When the defense questioned him about the statement that he "got the impression she wanted to go to bed" with him, Mr. Miller replied, "Well she never really said anything about it. I just felt like that was what she wanted!"

What was it with him? She was flirtatious and touchy, so it automatically meant "take me to bed?" My mother always told me that I did not know the difference between being friendly and being flirtatious, but if touching a leg during conversation was the universal signal for "take me to bed," my life would have been a lot more exciting!

I could not imagine this boy refusing any offer or refraining from putting a move on Patricia if he had even the slightest ounce of encouragement! Trust me — I saw this guy!

"Mr. Miller, how did you know Mr. Wagger was intoxicated?"

"Well, I could smell alcohol on his breath, and he was very belligerent."

"Why did you think there was going to be a fight?"

"Well, I had saw him in this condition before, drunk I mean! It always ended with him beating his wife and kids."

Ah! At last! Someone who could substantiate the accusations of abuse!

My guess is that Chad did not answer the defense's line of questions quite like the prosecution had hoped. There was no re-direct, and they had no further questions!

Next to take the stand was Upland County's own Mrs. Poole! Nothing went unnoticed by Kathy Golden. She had seen it all, knew it all, and today was willing to tell it all! Her testimony was about to become the defendant's worst nightmare — she would prove to be the most dangerous witness to date! Prosecutor Smith began.

"Kathy, how did you come to know the Wagger family?"

"I was living in an upstairs apartment at the Harald Apartments. I saw Patricia at many of the parties there. Most of the time she was drinking beer or some sort of alcohol when I saw her! The last party we attended together, I saw her leave with Wade Bradsworth. That was Friday, the week before the shooting. They left together at about 1:00. Jamie Benton and me were standing on the balcony when we saw Wade coming back from Patricia's house. That was about 6:00 in the morning. But this wasn't the only time I saw it happen. There was at least one other time I am sure of."

Dear God! Didn't these people ever sleep? No, I was sure, Kathy didn't!

Otherwise, she might miss something. She couldn't take a chance on somebody knowing something about a neighbor that they had not heard from her first.

I thought maybe the Benton person she was speaking of was related to the owner of the Tire Shop. If so, the relationship between he and Walter may have been more than just business.

Kathy continued, "One night after midnight, Patricia and Darlene came to my apartment and wanted me to run down the balcony with them with no clothes on. I wouldn't do it! They both got upset with me. I'm not that kind of person!"

Of course not! Maybe the defense couldn't say it, but I could think it! I would also bet that, according to Kathy, the only reason she attended those parties was to be the designated walker-home! I was anxious to see what the attention-minded defense attorney was going to do with Kathy.

"Kathy, you don't have any idea what took place between Wade Bradsworth and Mrs. Wagger do you?"

"No, I just assumed."

"Well, you do know what assuming means don't you?"

Good question, I thought, and he left it at that! I had to wonder how people ever got through life without the Kathy Goldens of the world. It was left up to people like her to make people like Patricia look far less than respectable.

I was more than relieved when the judge recessed until the next morning, not that going home made a lot of difference, though. I had so many questions! Other than Megan, I did not know whom I believed! Megan's testimony was so limited. I knew there was much more she could tell us, but was it fair to ask anymore of her? She had been very informative about the events leading up to the shooting, and she did not deny her role in the event. The one thing I did believe was that whatever led to the shooting of Walter Wagger had begun many years before. When the opportunity arose, the thoughts, the pain, the anger, and the need to stop it all came to an abrupt end. How quickly one's entire life can change, and without warning! One should never get too comfortable in a situation — it can change in the blink of an eye.

CHAPTER 11

I finally made it to my apartment with what I had chosen to leave behind, the trial and family in which I had become so wrapped up. Even on my way home, it weighed on my mind. I tried to watch television, but my thoughts kept going back to it. Once again, even my attempt to sleep was in vain. I was unable to decide where I stood!

I tried to picture the happenings that had transpired the weekend in question. What, after all that time, pushed Patricia over the edge? I tried to imagine the fear of being tortured in my own home; it must have been like a bad dream, only one from which they never awoke!

Patricia and those children must have felt like wild animals being chased from one end of a cage to the other, injured often, but never killed, constantly wondering when the next hunt would take place!

I tried to analyze what could have caused Walter to become so angry. Did his anger only flare when he was drinking? Was it jealousy that caused him to be so overtaken with violence toward his wife and kids? Deep down, I realized he must have been tortured by a demon within. When it was over, he always apologized. He was sorry from the first time it happened! But not sorry enough to get help and keep it from happening again. Maybe he was just unable to control his anger. But why didn't he try to get some help?

And why did she keep going back?

The prosecution had stated that he had threatened to kill her before but had not done so. She, on the other hand, had sought ways of stopping the abuse herself. What happened this time that was so different? Where would I find a happy medium, one small place to put it all into perspective?

There must have been something between them. For nine years, they stayed together. They had conceived three children. For nine years, the abuse continued. Surely, the magnitude of that abuse hinted that sooner or later somebody was going to die. And they must have known somebody would have to pay for that death. So why didn't somebody take the initiative to end it before it went so far?

When that death occurred, the physical pain ended!

I could tell from the way I was talking to myself and making no sense that it was too soon to draw any conclusions, but remaining neutral made no sense either. There was still too much testimony to be heard! We still had not heard from the defense. We still had not heard from Patricia's family. I wondered how they were feeling about her now. Had they stood beside her in the wake of her victory from abuse, a tragedy within itself? I felt certain that when we heard them speak, we would be presented with the good side of this woman. She could not be all bad!

She had four healthy children! She had never been arrested, even on a public intoxication charge. Within a few hours, we would begin yet another day of the trial, and I knew the defendant was getting closer to the stand. Maybe then, I could reach my conclusion.

CHAPTER 12

This was my first real experience in the courtroom, so each day was filled with learning, and I was most anxious to attend every session. Upland County Sheriff Frank Gossett was now taking the stand in what the prosecution called its final witness. Without a doubt, he would prove to be the most crucial witness for the prosecution, with the exception of Megan.

Sheriff Gossett had taken the statement from Patricia, after the death of Mr. Wagger, on February 27, 1987.

"She said the shooting took place at her home about 1:00 in the morning. Patricia said, 'Walter came home about 11:30 and said, "Bitch, I thought I told you not to be here." He kicked me as soon as he walked in the door. Then he went into the kitchen and told Megan to get out of his God damned way. He hit Megan, then he fixed him a drink and came back into the living room. He started calling me names. He sat down in the chair and told me to fix him something to eat before he finished beating my brains out.'"

Sheriff Gossett was a soft-spoken man. The slightest movement in the courtroom made it difficult to hear him. With the exception of the time frame, so far, the statement Patricia had given to him coincided with Megan's testimony. There was so much to consume at this moment! I didn't want to miss the tiniest particle of information. For the first time, we were going to hear the defendant's version of what had taken place, or at least her story after the smoke had cleared!

Sheriff Gossett continued to read the defendant's statement verbatim: "'I had Megan to fix him something to eat because my arms were too sore from the beatings. By the time Megan got his food fixed, he was madder than ever. He slapped the plate of food on the floor. He told Megan to pick up the plate.

55

Then he passed out in the chair. I told Megan to go into the bedroom and get my gun from under the pillow. I told her then to turn off the living room light. Megan did, and she put her coat over the gun so if Walter woke up he wouldn't see it.'

"Mrs. Wagger said she kept thinking about how he had beat her up and called her names. How he had hit her mother and Megan. How he had forced her into the bedroom with a butcher knife, and how he had choked her. She said Megan went to bed, and she woke her up."

"'Megan asked me if I had shot him, and I told her I couldn't do it. Megan said she could do it cause she hated him.'

"Mrs. Wagger admitted to me that she knew it was wrong, but she told Megan to go ahead. She saw it as her only way out.

"'I couldn't leave because he had both sets of car keys! I was afraid if he woke up, he was going to kill me. Megan took the gun and went into the living room. I stayed in the kitchen and covered my ears, but nothing happened. Megan came running in there and said the gun wouldn't fire. I took the gun and pulled the bolt back to make sure there was a bullet in it. I shoved the bolt back and over, then gave it back to Megan, telling her to pull harder on the trigger. She went back into the living room. I stayed in the kitchen and put my hands back over my ears. Again, nothing happened! She came back into the kitchen and told me the gun wouldn't shoot. This time I checked the safety and it was off. I gave the gun back to Megan and told her to pull harder. I stayed in the kitchen with my ears covered, and this time she shot him.'"

Gasps of disbelief echoed through the courtroom. If she had premeditated killing her husband before, she was certainly more determined than ever. It was then that I realized that if she really wanted him dead, she could have taken this action a long time ago. After nine years, this woman had reached her breaking point! Dear God, don't let it be that she purposely used her daughter! Sheriff Gossett continued as Prosecutor Marks asked him if Mrs. Wagger ever told him when she loaded the gun.

"She said it was earlier that morning when she loaded the gun and took it into Megan's bedroom. She put it under the pillow! She said she knew if she got the chance, she was going to do it. She said she didn't have the nerve to do it, and Megan had already said she would. When she told Megan to go ahead, she hated him for what he had done to her, and she wanted him dead."

"Did Mrs. Wagger tell you why she told a different story to the officers who were on scene the morning of the shooting?"

"She said she was scared. Scared because she didn't know what would happen to her. She was taking up for Megan too. She admitted to me that she had told Megan what she should tell the police about the shooting. She said, 'I figured they wouldn't take me to jail, or Megan either cause she's just a kid. I figured they wouldn't do nothing to me if Megan shot him.'"

The Sheriff continued: "She didn't feel she had done anything wrong. She thought he was going to kill her if he woke up and she was still there. It was just a matter of time. The way Mrs. Wagger saw it, it was self-defense. But then she said, 'I'm not glad he is dead. I loved him. But what I done seemed to be the only way out.'"

In cross-examination, Sheriff Gossett stated that he was unaware of any calls made to his department by Mrs. Wagger during the weekend before the shooting.

"Sheriff Gossett, did you ask Mrs. Wagger during that statement why she didn't leave?"

"Yes! But I did not inquire as to whether or not Mr. Wagger had taken both sets of keys to the vehicle with him when he left."

The defense had no further questions.

Sheriff Gossett then took his pre-assigned seat to the right of the two prosecuting attorneys. I knew we had not heard the last from him.

Prosecutor Marks then stood to face the judge.

"The State rests, Your Honor!"

The time was approximately 3:20 on the afternoon of June 17!

I thought to myself how we would now have to sit and listen to Patricia telling the same story. What I had waited so long to hear seemed as if it would be useless at this time. My first instinct was to take the ten-minute recess to become unattached. I was never going to find that happy medium. In my eyes, there was more than one victim. The one who was shot, the one who did the shooting, and the one who was responsible! Three victims, one cause! It was all there, but something brought me back to my seat. Something, or someone!

Defense Attorney Ray made a motion before the beginning of Patricia's side.

"Your Honor, the defense moves to strike evidence on behalf of the State to direct the jury to return a verdict of not more than voluntary manslaughter for the reasons that the State has failed to prove either first- or second-degree murder or the intent of premeditated murder."

Judge Kimble, who we had heard so little from, denied the motion, sighting the grounds that Megan had testified that her mother, the defendant, had asked her to shoot Mr. Wagger, that her mother did load the gun, and checked it three times, sending her daughter back into the living room each time to shoot Walter Wagger.

"Mr. Ray, your motion is denied!"

I did not envy the jury in this case. When the trial first began, I felt it must be a real honor to be seated up there, knowing that the final decision in the most publicized trial in Upland County lay in your hands. Knowing that, for the next few days, they, as the chosen few, held a woman's freedom in their hands. But deep down, I would not have traded places with any one of them, not for love or money, to know, when this was over, that I had made a decision that would affect a mother and four children for the rest of their lives. But in spite of it all, it was their duty, and each one had to agree on the decision — beyond any reasonable doubt! From where I was seated, it was impossible. I redundantly thanked God that I was not one of them.

CHAPTER 13

Defense Attorney Carl Ray was about to take the spotlight as he introduced his first witness.

Olen Templeton, an elderly man, had been a landlord to the Wagger family in Greenberg County. Patricia and Walter lived there with their son, Colin, from an unknown date in 1979 to 1980.

"Mr. Templeton, can you tell us what you observed as far as the treatment of Patricia Wagger by her husband, Walter, while they resided at that residence?"

"Seemed like a damned war to me. One time, well many times, Patricia came to our house with her mouth swollen and bleeding. She had been kicked out of her own home, in the rain and snow, by that so-called husband. She would bring that little baby up to our house, and my wife, she thought she was a doctor you know, would patch her up and stuff. I never actually saw him beat his wife, but I know I saw her all mangled up. He drank a lot! I saw that lots of times. I finally had to make them leave the trailer. Shortly after that, I guess, he got transferred some place else."

In cross-examination, Mr. Templeton stated he never actually saw the Waggers fighting, "but God knows I could hear them, and that was almost every day."

"Mr. Templeton, do you know of any other medical treatment Mrs. Wagger received other than from your wife?"

"No, just from her!"

"Did you ever see Mrs. Wagger with any other men, other than her husband?"

"No indeed, I did not!"

He was done.

Mr. Templeton's daughter, Peggy Jordan, lived on the property adjacent to the Wagger home during the time they rented off her father. She testified to having never seen Mr. Wagger hit his wife, but she had seen Patricia with indications of having been struck.

"It was at my father's house. I saw her numerous times with black eyes, bruises, and bloody. I often heard Walter use profanity toward his wife; her daughter, Megan; and his mother-in-law."

It was what the defense needed from her, and I thought it was looking quite good! With two defense witnesses down, they had established proof that the abuse had been ongoing. But, thanks to cross-examination, we were soon back to square one.

Prosecutor Marks managed to take the same questions asked by Defense Attorney Ray, put them in a different context, and get totally different answers.

He was starting to make these defense attorneys look like amateurs.

Peggy was saying to Prosecutor Marks that she had never seen Mr. Wagger hit Patricia or Megan and was not aware of any medical treatment Patricia had received as a result of the beatings.

"The arguments between them seemed to occur when he was drinking and seemed to be worse when her daughter and mother came to visit. I had seen all of them with bruises, but to be honest with you, I can't say who put them there."

Yes. She had speculated! But the prosecution wanted only the facts.

So now, the only proven facts were that the Waggers had argued and Patricia, Megan, and Mrs. Billingston had all been seen with bruises on them, but there were only guesses as to who was responsible for those bruises. Definitely abuse, but who was at fault?

Why didn't she ever go to the hospital? Why didn't she ever report this man to the authorities? So many whys and so few answers!

I thought maybe I was just thinking too far ahead. My only hope, and Patricia's, too, for that matter, lay in the prospect that the defense might have a plan to turn this thing around and pull it off. If they did have one, they sure as hell were keeping it a secret!

For the moment, the proof, beyond a reasonable doubt, that Walter abused his wife was thrown completely out of the water, as Prosecutor Marks objected to the very first question to the next witness, Jack Mason, attorney at law.

"Mr. Mason, do you have an opinion as to what kind of mother Patricia

Wagger was?"

Judge Kimble sustained the objection on the grounds that Mr. Mason could not possibly know what took place inside the Wagger home.

"Mr. Mason, when did you first meet Patricia Wagger?"

"In February 1980. Mrs. Wagger had a consultation of a domestic matter. She came to me asking about the chances of a divorce being granted in her favor. She stated there had been violence in the home and she had a bad home life. She was not happy and wanted out before it got worse. I told her what her chances were and that it was mandatory that she prove such allegations in order for a divorce to be granted in her favor."

"Did you ever hear from her again?"

"In September 1985, she contacted me in reference to a title exam being completed on property she and her husband were hoping to purchase in Farmtown. That exam was never completed, and she never returned to my office for divorce proceedings."

This time it hit like a brick! Every time Patricia began to let people know what was happening within the walls of her home, letting them know what the real Walter was like, he packed her up and moved her elsewhere, probably promising her a nicer home and a better life! He would remain at that location until she found someone else to confide in and his heinous behavior became public! Then, without warning, the move was on.

And with that, another day was complete!

I began paying more attention to the defendant the next day. Only a few short days before, she had a life! Even if it was haphazard with this trial hanging over her head. She was working at a nursing home, the best job she had known, and it was a chance to start over. She had found friends in those she worked with, and for the first time in months, she had actually laughed!

A year ago, she had been, without a doubt, responsible for a crime. Not just a misdemeanor, but murder! She had accepted that responsibility. The weekend leading up to the murder had been long. For better than seventy-two hours, she listened as accusations flew from the man who claimed he loved her. The man she loved. She watched as the anger built and the name-calling turned into beatings.

Walter had blamed Patricia for the jeep being wrecked and accused her of sleeping with other men.

According to testimony, she had sought help but there was "nothing anyone could do." She had cried, pleaded, and prayed, but nothing worked. She couldn't sleep for fear of not waking up. She couldn't take care of her children for the pain he had caused. Something had to give!

She knew somebody was going to die, and she would be damned if it was going to be her or the children. At last, I was able to put myself in her shoes! The only question I had now was why it had taken so long to take action. Why had it come to this? Why did she not just do it herself? I was now more anxious than ever to hear her side of the story. However, my heart ached for her and her children.

That night, as I lay sleeping, or at least trying to sleep, in my own bed, those babies were lying awake, wondering what was going to happen to their mother and the sister who had taken on the same role — Patricia, isolated in the Upland County jail, and Megan in a strange bed away from the other children. Colin, Michelle, and Michael were, by the grace of God, together, but now they were only a family of three!

She had plenty of time to think about the murder, but it was too late to take it back.

CHAPTER 14

The next day of the trial began with defense witness Cindy Blake, yet another resident of the Harald Apartments. She was not hesitant when the question was thrown at her asking if Walter Wagger was an abusive man.

"I was at Delores Losh-Moria's apartment at approximately 6:00 on Monday before the shooting when Walter came over. He came into her apartment very angry. He wanted to know who his wife was sleeping with. Delores told him nothing! He told her if she didn't tell him he was going to kill her and his wife. He said eventually he would find out! Delores still never said anything. Walter then shoved Delores and left. Later that evening, he came back over to her apartment and told me to leave because he wanted to talk to Delores in private. I told him it wasn't his apartment, and if Delores wanted me to leave, she would tell me to go. Delores told me not to leave so I stayed there. Walter got mad at Delores again and called her a stupid bitch, then he knocked her over the bar."

"Cindy, how long have you known Patricia Wagger?"

"I guess about two years. But we were never allowed to be friends because Walter said I was a bad influence on her. He wouldn't let me visit or nothing, so we just talked at the get-togethers and stuff."

"Did you ever see Patricia with any bruises?"

"Yes, but Patricia told me she did not know how she got them."

I was curious as to why Patricia had protected this monster — a creature with no conscience! Maybe she was happy in this place, and if word got around that Walter abused her and the children — and word does travel fast — they would once again fall into the routine of moving. In an odd sort of way, she really did have friends, people who knew what occurred when Walter was home, but until this incident, never made comment or passed judgment. They allowed her to be herself — that one person Walter never knew!

Prosecutor Marks asked only three simple questions of Ms. Blake.

"Cindy, did you ever hear rumors, or had you reason to believe, that Mrs. Wagger was having an affair with Wade Bradsworth?"

"I had heard rumors, but as far as I was concerned, it was only rumors."

"Did you see Mrs. Wagger with any bruises that weekend?"

"Well, she didn't get out of the house much that weekend. But Sunday night, after Walter brought her over to the apartment building, I saw bruises on her then."

"Cindy, one final question: why didn't you ever tell anyone about the bruises you saw on Mrs. Wagger?"

"I didn't think it was any of my business."

Good answer! Unfortunately, that was the way most people felt, and that could have been a contributing factor in this case. Cindy was not like most of the witnesses who had testified; it was as if she knew too much.

Prosecutor Marks then stated that he had subpoenaed Cindy, and she could not be excused, nor could she remain in the courtroom. What was he up to? What else could she possibly know to tell that would benefit the prosecution? It would be days before we found out!

CHAPTER 15

In my eyes, Walter Wagger was becoming more of a mongrel with each passing day! I meant no ill sentiment to the dead, but even though he died at the age of twenty-nine and in the prime of his life, he left quite a legacy behind.

In the defense's opening statement, Walter was described as a terrorist in his own home. That statement was beginning to make more sense with each testimony, but no one could make him out to be more of a bastard than Megan herself already had, and that was enough proof for me.

While I sat in my rather hard section of a bench in the courtroom, I became more impatient to hear the defendant's testimony. I began to wonder if I was truly ready for her version of the nightmare. Walter was abusive. He had made life for his wife, three children, and his stepdaughter a living hell. How much worse could it get?

From day one of the trial, Walter had been described as an insurgent. More witnesses had come to his defense than had not. I wanted to become numb and forget the personal feelings I had acquired, to uphold my oath taken many years ago as a news reporter, to cover each story without prejudice! All I wanted to do was write the best news story I possibly could and inform the audience of what was happening without boring them. I wanted to show no emotion, sort of like a member of the jury. But by now, it was too late!

I had certainly become biased, but each testimony gave me a prejudice toward one of the three involved! In my mind, there was more than one victim. Honestly, the child had been my main concern from the time she sat on that stand.

The testimonies were ready to continue!

Delores Losh-Moria, another Harald Apartment resident, was next to take her place on the witness stand. She considered herself not just any resident, but Patricia's friend, in spite of Walter's wishes. She looked toward Patricia and gave her a nod, as if to assure her she would give it her best shot.

"Ms. Losh-Moria, how long have you known Patricia Wagger?"

"Since the last part of December 1985!"

"Did you ever see any signs of abuse by her husband?"

"Yes! Lots of times!"

"Did you ever hear the rumors about Patricia and Wade Bradsworth?"

"Yes! But to tell you the truth, everybody slept with everybody at the Harald Apartments. But I never saw Patricia with any other men other than at parties."

Delores corroborated Cindy's story about Sunday, when Walter came to her apartment twice, looking for answers and leaving with none.

"Did you see Walter anymore that night after he knocked you over the bar?"

"Yes. That night about 11:00, I saw him on the balcony at the Harald Apartments. He was drunk, and he said he was going over to the house and was going to beat the hell out of Patricia if she didn't fix him something to eat. That was the last time I saw him before he died."

"When did you learn about Walter's death?"

"You mean the death or the shooting?"

"Well, let's start with the shooting."

"Well, I was in the midst of all the commotion at their house that morning, but it wasn't until later that day when I talked to Patricia about it."

"When did that happen?"

"After the police officers and ambulance left, Patricia came over to my apartment. She was crying! Then the kids came over later."

"Did you notice Patricia and Megan talking between themselves after they came to your apartment?"

"No, they didn't talk at all."

I found that to be rather odd. When did they concoct the story both told to the news reporter and the officer the following day? Were they mad at each other for what had taken place? Had they found the time to think about what they had done together, and, with deep regret, one was silently blaming the other? Why didn't they talk?

In cross-examination, the prosecution found that this witness would not sway. Delores was telling the truth as she knew it. She was being very careful not to allow Mr. Marks to turn that truth around, as Mr. Marks had been known to do just that — discredit those who had taken Patricia's side as if their lifestyles did not discredit them enough. Delores wore an expression of fear; she was afraid it might not come out just right! With one slip of the tongue, her credible testimony could easily be misconstrued. Even a year later, it was evident that Delores's picture of the event in question was still quite clear as she continued.

"Patricia didn't act any different toward other men when Walter was away than when he was home. She loved him! She just got tired of being beat all the time."

"Ms. Losh-Moria, didn't you place a couple of phone calls from Mr. Carder's apartment for Mrs. Wagger?"

"Yes, to Minnerstown Medical Center. They told me Walter was in bad shape, and they needed someone from his immediate family to come up and sign a statement so they could operate on him. But I told them Patricia didn't have a way up. I talked to them three times, and the last time they told me Walter had died on the operating table. I told them to tell his wife, so Patricia got on the phone and they told her."

The prosecutor, for some reason, chose to stop the questioning at that point, leaving the rest of the story to the defense.

"Delores, what did Patricia do when the doctor told her Walter had died?"

"She kept saying, 'God, I can't believe it's true.' Then she threw down the phone and ran outside and down the balcony. I got back on the phone, and the doctor told me to get her. So we went down and got her! She said she was going to kill herself. She started hitting her fists against a trailer that was parked outside beside the apartments. We finally got her back into the apartment, and she said, 'I can't believe he is dead. What am I going to do without him?'"

I guessed that the reality of the shooting was then coming to life for Patricia.

"Delores, did you ever talk to Patricia or Megan about the shooting?"

"Yes, later that morning at my apartment. Megan asked Patricia if she should tell me that she shot her daddy, Walter! Patricia told Megan to be quiet. Then Megan told me what happened!"

"And what did Megan tell you?"

"She told me that Walter had been beating on them for two days. He had put a butcher knife to her mom's throat and shoved her into the bedroom. She said he was going to kill her and she was scared he would. So when Walter passed out in the chair, she shot him."

Prosecutor Marks then took the opportunity to pick up where he left off in his previous cross-examination.

"Delores, I have some letters here. I would like you to look at them and tell me if you have ever seen these letters."
As Delores looked over the letters, her eyes welled up with tears. I knew this was not going to be pleasant for either Patricia or Delores.

"Yes. These are letters Patricia wrote to her mother. After the shooting, they were given to me to keep."

"Would you please read paragraph three from the first letter to this court?"

"'Mom, would you get me some rat poison or send me some money to buy some? Walter is so mean, even to Colin, no bigger than he is!'"

"Delores, weren't you supposed to give me these letters?"

"Yes, but I didn't want to get involved!"

The defense then objected to the prosecution's request to have Delores read further information from the letters, stating that Delores had not written them and they had been sent to Evelyn Billingston, not her.

Judge Kimble sustained the objection.

I knew we had not heard the last of these letters. Jumping from witness to witness and topic to topic was certainly giving us a lesson in patience. Mrs. Billingston had not appeared on the witness stand, nor had the defendant.

There were no further questions, and Delores was excused.

Delores had been quite helpful to Patricia, for whatever reason. Somewhere along the line, Patricia had found a friend in Delores. That friend had just taken the routine of this trial and turned it around. She was going to tell the truth, and that truth could only give Patricia motive in the shooting of Walter. Delores was determined to prove that the abuse had taken place and she had witnessed it, right up until the night before Walter died!

It must have seemed like an eternity for Delores on that stand, all eyes on her. She must have been terrified! Prosecutor Marks had tried, but she did not falter. On re-direct, Delores still did not waver, and the question of whether or not the abuse had occurred in that home no longer existed.

CHAPTER 16

Spectators were taking time between witnesses to discuss the important elements of the trial. The only truth people seemed to identify with and fully believe in was Megan's testimony. I realized, even with all they had heard, their opinions had not changed one bit since the beginning of the trial.

I had to grin as many talked during breaks about being tired and what to have for dinner, wishing it was over, yet making plans to call someone the next morning to make sure they did not miss getting "the good seats."

Most of the people lined up the next day were the same faces I had seen since day one. These people knew less about the defendant than did I. Same time, same place, different day, there they were, hoping she would take the stand and come closer to the end they had already predicted.

We had listened to testimony that Patricia Wagger was very familiar with the local 911 system, having used it on several occasions, seeking help in an effort to stop the abuse from her husband, Walter. The last time was when she called to announce Walter had been shot.

Karen Cortney was regarded as the best at her job — Chief Dispatcher for the Upland County Communication Center, a system that was in the early stages and was one of the first in the state!

Karen was called as the next witness.

"Karen, can you describe how the Communication Center works?"

"Upon each call that comes into the center, we immediately ascertain the caller's name and the address and phone number from where they are calling."

"Are these calls recorded?"

"Yes, all calls that come into the center are recorded."

"Ms. Cortney, can you tell us when you received the first call from Patricia

Wagger on the weekend leading up to February 27?"

"On February 25th, a call came into the Comm Center — signal ten, which is the police code for a drunk. The party calling stated that his neighbor was beating up his wife and kids and then hung up. The caller did not give a name, but I took it as a younger male caller. The location was the community of Appleton, and the phone number matched that of the Wagger residence."

"What did you do with the information you had gotten from the caller?"

"I advised Deputy Knicely and Deputy Holten of the Upland County Sheriff's Department."

"Do you recall what time you got the call?"

"I gave the call to the Deputies at about 12:52 am."

"Do you recall any other calls your center received from that area during that weekend?"

"Yes, that same night, just minutes after the first call. At 12:57, Darlene Mason called the center and stated that Mr. Wagger was beating up his wife and trying to push her over the balcony. I then notified the deputies again. Then, at 1:07, Patricia Wagger called and said couples outside the Harald Apartments were fighting. I notified the deputies once more, and they said they were en route to the area."

"Did you receive any other calls from the Wagger home or Harald Apartments that you are aware of?"

"That night, at 10:52, Patricia Wagger called the Comm Center asking to speak with an officer. She said her husband was beating up on her and the kids."

"Do you have that message recorded?"

"No, Sir. For some reason that message was never taped."

"Do you know why that message was never recorded?"

"Well, it is my opinion the cassette was either bad or that message had been taped over."

On cross-examination, Prosecutor Smith asked Ms. Cortney to play back the call received at the Comm Center in the early morning hours of February 27." The tape was played:

"'This is Patricia Wagger, and I just shot my husband, Walter Wagger.'
'Where are you calling from?'
'Appleton.'
'What is your name? Your phone number?'
'742-0909.'
'Hold on while I transfer your call.'"

End of tape!

"Ms. Cortney, who was that call transferred to?"

"The call was transferred to the Upland County Sheriff's Department and the Upland County Emergency Squad for response."

The tape recording of the transfer was then played. After three rings, the call was received by the Upland County Emergency Squad.

"'This is Patricia Wagger. I need you out here! I just shot my husband!'

'Where do you live?'

'Appleton, across from the Harald Apartments!'"

The voice on the tape was very shaky! I glanced over at the defendant, and for the first time, I saw her express emotion. She began to wipe the tears, and I began to feel a knot forming in my throat, that same knot I felt when Megan began to talk about the shooting. I suddenly felt that this was not what she really intended to do. With all the calls for help and the different ways she had tried to end the abuse, it was a last minute thought. But then again, she had pre-loaded the gun and hid it in a safe place. Maybe she felt that, since no one had answered all the cries before, they wouldn't respond this time either. Maybe she felt no one would care anymore about Walter being shot than they had about her and the children being beaten by him. But I had been in the news far too long and knew within myself that, when it came to guts and glory, we all respond.

As questioning by the prosecution continued, Ms. Cortney stated that it was not unusual to receive calls from the Harald Apartments. This series of calls began in the early morning hours of February 25th, just after Walter arrived home from his job. She stated there had been no real indication that the Wagger family had been involved in the fighting. There were no other activities involving the Wagger family notated on the Comm Center logs until the shooting.

Wait a minute! The first call she received was from the Wagger residence, stating that the husband was beating up on his family. Then Darlene called, advising that Walter was trying to push his wife over the balcony. Now if that didn't involve the Wagger family, what in the hell warranted involvement? But the defense did not question the witness any further. Was I the only one who caught the discrepancy here? Or was I the only one who cared?

I was still very much puzzled as to why the deputies did not respond to the calls in the early morning hours of February 25th. Deputy Knicely had stated on the witness stand that he recalled getting only one call from the Wagger family that weekend. He spoke with Mrs. Wagger and advised her that, if her

71

husband was not home, beating on her at that moment, there was nothing he could do!

It seemed to me that, in light of the current testimony, by the early morning hours of February 27th, she was running out of choices!

I understood how receiving so many calls from the same location would become monotonous. The commotion was probably over once law enforcement got on scene, with everyone claiming to know nothing about what had happened. But isn't that why we have local law enforcement officers — to protect and to serve?

The trial was becoming monotonous as well. The only difference in the line of questioning teetering from the defense to the prosecution was that they were on opposite sides of the tracks. At this point, I would not bet the farm on either side. I had to wonder if the jury was having as much difficulty as I was in deciding the case. The only real difference was that my inhibitions were not going to matter.

CHAPTER 17

It was an ongoing bout between the defense and prosecution, trying to prove whose witnesses were the most reputable! Whose testimonies were more likely to convince the jury!

Reverend Claude McMillihen, Minister of the New Commandment Mission in Upland County, was next on the defense list to take the oath.

"Do you swear to tell the truth, the whole truth, and nothing but the truth, so help you God?"

"I do!"

He was a tall man wearing a face that was more than peaceful – it was a face solemn with truth! He bore the resemblance of the reverends portrayed in biblical times. His salt-and-pepper hair made his appearance quite distinguished, and his pale blue eyes stood out among his other characteristics. His was a sad, almost worrisome look!

He began: "My first encounter with the Wagger family was about two years ago when they first moved to the community. I always try to visit new families and invite them to my church. Mrs. Wagger allowed the children to attend; I transported them back and forth."

Mr. Ray continued his line of questioning.

"Reverend McMillihen, when did you first learn of the shooting of Walter Wagger?"

"I received a call from one of the residents at the Harald Apartments telling me of the incident. It was in the late morning hours that day. I, along with my wife, went to the Wagger home. Upon our arrival, I saw the television news reporter and several other folks standing around. The news reporter was talking to Megan and Colin. I went over to Mrs. Wagger, who was extremely upset at the time."

"Reverend McMillihen, did you observe any signs of physical abuse on Mrs. Wagger or the children?"

"Yes! Mrs. Wagger had bruises on her upper chest and shoulder. I convinced her to go the hospital. My wife and I took her and the children to St. Jacob's Hospital."

"Reverend McMillihen, did you, over the past two years, ever talk with the Wagger children about Walter?"

"Not directly. Often, I noticed fear in Megan and Colin when Mr. Wagger was home. Numerous times Megan indicated that she did not want to go home after the church service when Mr. Wagger was there. She would often say, 'I hope my step-father isn't home.' We let her speak, but we never asked any questions."

Reverend McMillihen spoke with such conviction for this family.

"Did Walter ever accompany the children to church?"

"No, he never attended the service. I only spoke with him a couple of times during the time they lived in the community. The first time, I invited him to church. He stated that he didn't care if Megan came to church, but he, his wife, and their children would not be attending. The next time I talked with him, he called and asked me to come over. He wanted to talk to me about attending church. By the time I arrived, he said he had changed his mind."

Through cross-examination, he further explained his involvement with the Wagger family and Megan after Walter was shot.

"I arrived at the home about 10:30 on the morning of February 27th. We took Mrs. Wagger and the children to the hospital in mid-afternoon. We waited at the hospital for about two hours before Megan and Mrs. Wagger were able to see a doctor. My wife and I waited until they had been examined and then took them back home."

It was no assumption on my part that Reverend McMillihen was truly a man of God. I recalled when he first encountered Megan in the courtroom. He walked in with people staring, her eyes lit up, and she ran to him, throwing both arms around his waist and gripping as tight as one could imagine. The smile on her face told a story!

The question was raised by many as to who this man was. The child who many had kept a watchful eye on was running to him with outstretched arms; she never stopped until she reached him, holding on like she had never been hugged before. He returned the hug without letting go until her fragile arms let loose. This man seemed to be the only reinforcing adult figure in her life!

After letting go of the reverend, Megan embraced the tall, attractive, younger woman standing behind him. We now knew who that man was, and with the next witness, we soon found out the name of the woman.

Defense Attorney Ray began his questioning of the very humble, very fragile, very honest Jane McMillihen.

"Mrs. McMillihen, can you tell us of any conversation you had with the Wagger children on the ride to St. Jacob's Hospital on February 27, 1987?"

"The two children, Megan and Colin, rode in the back of the truck with me. They sat in silence for the most part, neither of them saying anything to each other. Then finally, Colin said 'Megan, I hate you! You shot my daddy!' Then Megan said to me, 'Miss Jane, it's my fault! He didn't like me. Most of the fights were because of me and Grandma.'"

Mrs. McMillihen's eyes began to fill with tears. She waited briefly before continuing.

"I told her it was not her fault that her mom and step-father fought or that her step-father drank. Then it got silent again."

I could picture this woman trying to save these children, trying to salvage whatever peace and love had not died with Walter, trying to help them hold on to whatever this family had left.

"Mrs. McMillihen, was there any other conversation between you and the children?"

"After a few minutes, Megan told me she just knew somebody was going to die, and she didn't want it to be her mom or one of the other kids or her grandma, so she shot him!"

Megan was continuously ringing her hands as Mrs. McMillihen testified, just as she had all of the other times she was upset or nervous. I knew the testimony was really bothering her.

My mind went racing back to when Megan was on the stand, constantly wringing her hands and biting her bottom lip.

"Mrs. McMillihen, did Megan or Colin ever talk to you about their home life?"

"One night at church, Colin asked me if my husband and I ever got mad at each other. I said yes. Then he asked me, 'Does Brother Claude ever cuss at or hit you?' I said no and asked him if his daddy ever did that. He told me yes, but not all the time."

"Mrs. McMillihen, did you ever see the children with bruises on them?"

"Yes! I saw them two or three times a week, and many times they had bruises on them."

75

In answering the lone question by the prosecution, Mrs. McMillihen stated she never really saw the physical abuse occur, and the children didn't seem to want to talk about it much, so she never asked any questions.

I thought of how so many suspected, but nobody wanted to ask.

Mrs. McMillihen then left the witness stand and took her seat in the courtroom beside her husband. The two were in the courtroom everyday after that. I felt it was for support rather than to hear the indiscretions and have something to gossip about during recess. By watching the husband and wife team, one could easily see why the Wagger children had become so fond of and trusted them. Brother Claude, as they called him, sat with his arm around Miss Jane. When the testimony became a little harsh, he would squeeze her hand. In watching them, I knew their love was a Godsend! They possessed what many search for a lifetime and never find.

The court was about to close for the noon recess when thirteen-year-old Audrey Dillon took the stand. She attended school with, and was very much a friend to, Megan.

"Audrey, did Megan ever talk to you about her home life?"

"Well, she often told me she was tired of her step-father beating on her mother and the kids. She said if she ever got the chance, she was going to kill him."

"Did you believe her?"

"At first I thought she was just talking tough, but then she told me how she would do it."

"And what did she say about that?"

"She said she would wait until he went to sleep then stab him."

"Audrey, did you ever see Megan with bruises on her?"

"She always had bruises on her. One day I asked her where she got them, and she told me her step-father put them there."

Prosecutor Marks asked Audrey to elaborate on the times she saw bruises on Megan and the times Megan had talked about killing her stepfather.

"She had talked about killing him more than once. I saw bruises on her more than once. What I'm saying is that each time she came to school and talked about killing him, I could easily see the bruises on her."

There came that lump in my throat again! I pondered about these children. Would their life with Walter Wagger ever leave their mind? Would Megan ever be able to love or trust anyone? Would Colin grow up believing that beating was the way to control one's household? Would their childhood with Walter scar them for life?

My God! How could an eleven-year-old child, or even the younger children, know so much hatred? Colin had told Megan he hated her. Was anger already building up inside him, or did that just seem like the right thing to say as the world crumbled around them?

Yes, Walter was dead. But I believed the memories he left behind would last a lifetime in the minds of these children.

Court recessed until 1:00!

CHAPTER 18

I had watched each day for Megan to return to the witness stand. When she had not returned to the courtroom after her initial testimony, I could only assume she would be back. The time had come for her to be queried once more about the weekend in question.

She appeared a little more rested than she had her first day on the stand. Still fragile, still innocent! I wondered why she had to be put through this again. Every eye was upon her and every ear listening closely to every word she spoke. What else could she possibly add?

Mr. Ray began.

"Megan, you have already been sworn in. You are still under oath. I only have a couple of questions for you:

"Megan, do you remember talking with Darlene over at the apartments after the shooting?"

"Yes."

"Do you remember what you told her?"

"I told her I shot my daddy, Walter, and I hoped he died."

"Megan, did you really want him to die?"

"I really just wanted him to leave."

"Megan, you didn't get along with Walter. Do you know why?"

"He didn't like me!"

"Why did you want him to leave?"

"I hated him for the way he treated Mom and Grandma and the kids. I just wanted him to leave and never come back. But I never wanted him to die."

"No further questions, Your Honor."

Prosecuting Attorney Marks waited momentarily before standing to face the child again.

"Megan, would you have shot Walter had your mother not told you to?"

"No."

I was hoping this would be the last time Megan would have to appear front and center. This had to be such a strain on her! Reliving all the madness from her painful past. Her testimony was quite clear. To sum it all up, on the weekend leading up to the shooting, Walter had been drinking. He began beating on her and her mother. Her mother had asked her several times if she could shoot Walter. Finally, she said yes. When the time came, her mother handed her the gun and sent her into the living room to end the pain. It took three times, but she lived up to her promise.

In many ways, Megan was the savior! She, not her mother, had stopped the pain. The real question lay in who was responsible, not who was guilty.

Domestic violence was a new subject to me! Growing up in a family of eleven with both parents working, as one of the young children, I was pretty much taken care of by older brothers and sisters. I had never seen a husband abuse his wife, had never seen a parent beat on a child, and had never seen a child abused by a brother or sister, other than typical family squabbles! Oh sure, there were times we thought the punishments were killing us, but now I knew it was nowhere near what these children had seen or felt. Nothing compared to what this family had suffered! But I also knew there was nothing I would not have done to protect my family. I knew that now, but it was certainly nothing that ever crossed my mind at that age! I never dreamed I would be put in a position where I would need to save my family from such pain, much less use a gun to do it!

Family Marriage Counselor Helena Ryder was immediately recognized by the court as an expert witness, as the defense continued without delay. She began her testimony by describing the three types of violence that occurred in the home. Did Patricia suffer from the "Battered Woman Syndrome?" In Mrs. Ryder's opinion, she had!

"There are three types of violence that can occur in an abusive home: physical; sexual; and what we consider the most dramatic, psychological. Battered Woman Syndrome is defined as those who have characteristics of suffering from violence in the home. One such common characteristic is low self-esteem. This becomes a vicious cycle! The woman needs the man to feel appreciated. She will do whatever he deems necessary to please him so as not to be rejected. The man needs the woman to make him feel like a man. He must always feel like he is in complete control. When the violence occurs, she feels as if nobody understands and it is her fault. He feels justified in having taught her a lesson."

"Mrs. Ryder, why do they stay?"

"At first, they try to get out, but then after awhile, they just give up. This is what we term "learned helplessness." He becomes very jealous and starts accusing her of having an affair because he feels threatened. She feels responsible for him and his actions. The problem is not anger — it is the way it is used to handle the situation. After beating her, he will do whatever it takes to get her back. He threatens to take the children, and many times, that is all she has. She goes back because of helplessness, reinforcement, and fear for the children, as well as herself."

"Why don't they get help?"

"All too often, a woman will tell nobody about the situation due to the embarrassment and humiliation, and she certainly does not talk about it in front of the man for fear he will beat her again!"

I found a lot of my questions now being answered. Suddenly, it occurred to me that Patricia had given everything to this man. Absolutely everything! Her love, her devotion, her self-esteem, her children! She probably would have even sold her soul just to stop the pain. I understood why she had never left for good. She had nothing to go on and nothing to take. She had given it all to Walter, right down to the last minute!

This was a small town. Things like domestic violence did not exist! Or did it? Apparently, it had, but folks like me were exempt from being exposed to it. All too often, it was looked upon as a family matter and seldom reported, much less put out in the public eye. To me, this gave reason to the Wagger family's ongoing moves. This mess — the many years of hell — was beginning to make sense to me.

I could understand some of the symptoms in Megan: becoming angry and talking of killing. But what haunted me the most was her deep, integrated feeling of hatred!

The prosecution began a line of questioning, pushing Mrs. Ryder for her qualifications. I imagined this had something to do with Mr. Mark's objection to Mr. Ray's earlier question of whether Mrs. Ryder was qualified to testify on behalf of the Battered Woman Syndrome.

"I have worked on five separate criminal cases regarding the Battered Woman Syndrome. Two involved murder, two assault cases, and assisted in a murder case. Each case dealt with domestic violence!"

Shot that theory out of the water! There was no question she was qualified, so Mr. Marks continued.

"What type of evaluation did you perform on Mrs. Wagger?"

"On March 5, 1988, I performed a three hour evaluation on the defendant and on May 29, 1988, at which time I performed a one hour evaluation! These both consisted of question-and-answer type evaluations which required Mrs. Wagger to answer questions about her childhood and her life with Walter Wagger."

"And what did your evaluations conclude?"

"It is my opinion that Mrs. Wagger did suffer from the Battered Woman Syndrome."

"What about Megan?"

"Well, in a violent home, the eldest child will often assume the responsibility of the parent that is the victim. They have a tendency to become the confidant."

More and more, Mrs. Ryder was painting a clearer picture of that situation in the Wagger home. Everything she said seemed to fit the description of what went on inside. More and more, I liked the picture less and less.

It was time to move on.

At St. Jacob's Hospital, Patricia was examined by a young intern. Morgan Riff briefly described his encounter with Mrs. Wagger.

"It was approximately 3:30 in the afternoon on February 27, 1987. She told me she had suffered bruises from beatings by her husband on the two days prior to her visit at the emergency room. Upon examination, I discovered a small laceration inside her upper lip and bruises under her chin, on her right shoulder, on her hip, and on her pelvic bone. I also discovered abrasions on her neck, left shoulder, and chest area. Her foot and left ankle were swollen and had a bluish tint. She stated the injuries were sustained by her husband's fist and open hand. No weapon was used during the assault. She received no treatment at that time."

The testimony was beginning to run rampant through my head. This doctor was saying as little as possible. He seemed to be trying really hard to make the injuries appear minimal. What difference did it make?

It certainly was not self-defense! Walter was passed out when the shooting occurred. She had apparently been struck by somebody during the previous two days, but I had to wonder how much of those two days she could remember. I believed that, at some point, she did just give up, and from that point on, she knew nothing. But a guilty verdict by reason of giving up was not an option.

We were beginning to narrow down those who saw Patricia and Megan the day of the shooting. Registered Nurse Cecilia Norman was on duty at St. Jacob's Hospital on that day and assisted in the examination of Patricia.

"Cecilia, how did you find Mrs. Wagger when she arrived at St. Jacob's?"

"She was very withdrawn during this time. She said very little about the condition she was in, and I heard nothing from her about the shooting."

"What about Megan?"

"I noticed her being much more mature and experienced than most her age. She was very talkative with her mother. She seemed very protective of her mother."

I could see that over-protectiveness toward her mother when I listened to Megan testify. She had watched her mother be abused by the same man off and on for nine years, even more so in the past few months! That abuse was now over, and Megan intended to keep it that way.

The prosecution had no questions for Mrs. Norman.

As the day was drawing nearer to a close, Defense Attorney Ray wasted no time continuing.

"State your name, please."

"Dr. Charles Abrams."

"What is your occupation?"

"I am in private practice. I specialize in family medical practice."

"Dr. Abrams, have you ever treated Patricia Wagger?"

"Yes. On February 20, 1986, I treated her for pregnancy."

"Can you tell us about her visit to your office?"

"She came to see me and was very depressed. She was almost to the point of committing suicide!"

"Your Honor, I object!" came the words of Prosecutor Marks.

"On what grounds, Mr. Marks?"

"I find it difficult to qualify Dr. Abrams as a psychiatrist since he specializes in family practice. Therefore, I do not feel he is qualified to give a report on Mrs. Wagger's mental state at that time."

"Objection sustained!"

Attorney Ray took a deep breath, as if sustaining the objection was not justified. But everyone knows the judge rules, so Mr. Ray continued.

"Did you see Mrs. Wagger after that?"

"Yes. Almost a month later, she returned to my office. On March 21, 1986, she came back in. Again, she was depressed and stated that she really did not want to have another child. I asked her if she used any form of birth control. She said she had been using an IUD, but her husband wanted another child, so the IUD was removed. She stated that she had thought about having an abortion and telling her husband she was not pregnant. I then asked her not to do anything until she returned to my office."

Prosecutor Marks remained seated as he asked Dr. Abrams if he noted any bruises or abrasions on Mrs. Wagger during either visit.

"No. There was only one complete examination, and that was on March 21. After that when she came to visit, the only examination was performed on the abdomen."

The defense then asked Dr. Abrams if he knew whether Mrs. Wagger ever gave birth to that child.

"Yes. On September 20, 1986, I delivered her son."

Court recessed at the conclusion of Dr. Abram's testimony. It was now Friday, and another day was behind us. On what was a very rare occasion, Judge Kimble ordered the court to reconvene Saturday morning at 9:00.

I was personally pleased that I was not going to spend the weekend sitting at home thinking about what was going to take place Monday.

That night, I sat at home trying to put all of the day's testimony in some kind of order! There was so much to consume, and most of it was opinionated. It was just a matter of who and what one believed. With the exception of Megan, Deputy Maracos, and Dr. Ryder, the testimonies were one-sided — either for the defendant, or for the kind, wonderful, good-husband, good-father, Walter Wagger. I pretty much felt the sides were even. It was very difficult to relate to the domestic violence this family had known all too well. Many didn't believe it; some couldn't believe it; and the rest just didn't want to believe it — so they didn't!

CHAPTER 19

Saturday morning, June 17, 1988, at 9:00, the courtroom was congested. Today, I was seeing different faces. They had arrived early, and I almost had to forcibly remove a man from my assigned seat. By the time I arrived, had it not been for the cameras and my pass, I would have been standing in the hallway, like many who had waited all week for a spectator's kidneys to flare or the sudden urgency for nicotine to hit to find an empty seat.

Defense Attorney Carl Ray began day six of this well-publicized trial. Truthfully, it seemed like day one was a century past. The first witness to take the stand was Thomas White, a short, balding man in a business suit. He conducted himself in a business-like manner and was proud to show off his education. In fact, most of the time, he spoke over my head!

"Mr. White, what is your occupation?"

"I provide clinical and administrative services and am a counselor for the Summit Center in Greenberg."

"Did you ever have an occasion to meet with Patricia Wagger?"

"Yes, Sir. On February 18, 1983, I received a telephone call from Mrs. Wagger requesting services for her husband, Walter. She stated he was suffering from alcohol abuse. I set up a meeting with her, which occurred February 22, 1983. Mrs. Wagger arrived at the center with her husband, Walter."

"Can you give us a description of Walter Wagger?"

"He was 6'3" and weighed about two hundred and fifty pounds. He was a very loud man and often became obnoxious. He informed me the only reason he was at that meeting was to keep people off his back. He admitted to having only one problem; he said his drinking often got out of hand, but he was not an alcoholic."

"Mr. White, how long did the interview last?"

"I interviewed Mr. Wagger for about an hour and a half. During this interview, he became very violent, which proved to me he did have a very violent temper!"

"Did you interview Mrs. Wagger?"

"Not at that meeting. Her husband stated to me that when he was finished he was leaving."

"Did you meet with them again?"

"The next meeting I had with Mr. Wagger occurred exactly one month later, March 22."

"What occurred during this meeting?"

"It was not much different than the first one. He was constantly criticizing his wife, saying she was the root of the problem. He told me in this meeting that he drank to establish control. He stated his wife let the kids do whatever they wanted, and he had no control over his family, so when he drank he was able to gain that control. At the closing of the meeting, I told Mr. Wagger he needed to sign papers indicating he had received counseling through the Summit Center. However, he refused! He became very angry with me and tore up the papers I had handed to him. Then he left!"

"Were there any other meetings?"

"I later scheduled a meeting with both Mrs. and Mr. Wagger, who came to the center on April 1. I spoke with them separately. Mrs. Wagger was first. I asked her if any abuse took place within the household. At that time, she showed me a number of bruises he had given her. I then brought in Mr. Wagger, who found it necessary to over-shout his wife each time she attempted to speak. He told her she was not permitted to speak during these sessions — she was to sit there and keep her mouth shut. He indicated he was the man of the house, and no one was going to take that away. I then asked Mr. Wagger if he was having any success in controlling his drinking. He told me no. He further stated that he enjoyed drinking, and if he wanted to stop, he would do it without the help of me or his wife. He then abruptly walked out of the office and told me he would not be back. Mrs. Wagger stayed on, telling him she had left her jacket in my office. I then offered her the services of a domestic violence shelter."

Mr. White was a very distinguished-looking man whose intellect often became apparent in conversation. He sometimes lost me in that conversation, but he was adamant in giving his full description of the now-deceased Walter

Wagger. It struck me as somewhat bizarre that each time Patricia sought help, it occurred in the latter part of February. Each year, she sought help in a different way, but the month and days usually paralleled each other. I had to wonder if the month of February held some significance within this family.

"Mr. White, did you ever meet with the Waggers again?"

"No, Sir. Mr. Wagger called on April 18th and cancelled his appointment. He said his wife and kids were not home; he wanted to know where I was hiding them. I did not respond to him. He told me if they were not home soon he was going to come after me. I was unable to make contact with the Wagger family after that. In July 1983, I closed the case!"

"When was the next time you heard of this family?"

"When I heard about the shooting in the news."

"Did it surprise you?"

"No, Sir! I knew if they did not receive help with their problems, it was just a matter of time."

"Mr. White, the times Mr. Wagger came to see you and was not drinking, was he still violent and loud?"

"Yes. He was still domineering toward his wife. He was verbally abusive to her during those meetings. Mr. Wagger had been referred to me for alcoholism, something that caused him to become angry and violent, but that was not his only problem. Believe you me, Walter Wagger was the kind of man that, once you met him, you never forgot him!"

During cross-examination, Mr. White confessed, according to his records, that Walter had used the Summit Center once in August of 1984; however, he did not treat him. He also stated that Patricia was very negative toward her son, Colin. She said, "I don't know if I can think of anything good to say about him. He already is acting so much like his dad."

Mr. White left the witness stand without revealing whether or not Mrs. Wagger and her children had taken advantage of the shelter at the time Walter was trying to locate them. Confidentiality!

Day by day, the life of the Wagger family was becoming more complicated. There was no doubt this family had suffered from major abuse. All three types, based upon the testimony of Mrs. Ryder. From alcoholism to physical violence, these children had seen it all! The complicated question still remained: who was at fault? We would never learn of Walter's childhood, nor had we heard what prompted the drinking or the arguments. Was there ever a real reason for such anger?

I soon began feeling quite selfish. I wanted to hear it all! I had attended this trial everyday for totally selfish reasons — no regard to what this was doing to Patricia or the children and no regard for the family of Walter Wagger who had lost him suddenly, without warning, more than a year ago! Rehashing a time in Patricia and the children's life I was certain they would assume stay buried. They must have prayed that it was over! That night ended it! But each day, through the media, gossip, and the court system, they were all being forced to relive it. Not just the shooting, but the entire nine years that led up to that night. I wondered if, during the early days of Patricia and Walter, either of them had ever thought the abuse, alcoholism, and violence could cause such a scene — if either of them thought that what they tried so hard to keep hidden would ever bring about such public attention? To this family, it was all just a part of their everyday life, until those early morning hours when it became too much to endure!

The defense continued with a Child Protective Service worker for the local Department of Human Services. Joanna Thompson stated her first contact with the Wagger family was on October 27, 1986. She explained:

"I had been asked to do a follow-up on a case started by a previous employee on the Wagger family. Upon a referral, our first step is to conduct an interview with the children away from their parents. The initial interview had been done by the employee who worked the case before I did. I went to school and conducted my interview with Megan and Colin. The previous employee informed me that during her interview with the children, she learned some abuse had taken place. However, when I conducted my interview, I found no physical evidence at that time. In reading my notes, I stated that Colin said his parents did spank him when he had done something wrong. One time, he said he got a piece of cake when he wasn't supposed to, and his father spanked him and put black pepper in his eyes. I then asked him if his mother spanked him and he said, 'Usually she just yells.' I then interviewed Megan away from Colin. She said that Walter got really mad at Colin because he gave the finger to somebody. Walter took him into the house and started beating Colin's head against the wall. Later on that evening, I went to the Wagger residence and conducted an interview with Mrs. Wagger's mother. During that interview, both Mr. and Mrs. Wagger came home. Mrs. Billingston told them both about the child abuse allegations brought against them. At first, Walter became very belligerent, saying he spanked his children when they needed it. He said he was not going to let them go wild, but he did not beat them. He then wanted to know who had called. He began to tell me about all the pressure he was under. I completed my follow-up on the evening of October

27.”

The prosecution seemed quite interested in this witness. This could have possibly been the turning point in the trial. The children spoke of abuse, but more on the part of the wonderful Walter Wagger than on the part of their mother.

“The next time I came in contact with the family was on October 28. Walter called, saying his wife had left town with David Vincent, and he needed some help with the children. I offered to visit the home and talk with him, but he refused my services and said if he needed anything, he would call. I went to the home on the evening of November 24 and spoke with Mrs. Wagger, Mrs. Billingston, Megan, and Colin. All agreed that Walter had improved in his behavior. While I was there, Mr. Wagger came home. He was somewhat apprehensive and told me he did not need me, his wife had returned home. Mrs. Wagger told me she had just gone to pick up her mother and stayed a couple of days. I advised them to attend Parents Anonymous. Mr. Wagger told me he did not need it, but his wife was welcome to attend if she wanted. No action was taken on either parent, nor did either follow through with Parents Anonymous.”

I did not envy Mrs. Thompson's job. It had to be extremely strenuous. The important part, of course, would be the welfare of the children. All she really had to work with in this case were the parents working against each other, one child against the other, and the parents against the children. Everyone was entirely too scared to talk openly.

How could one determine what was right when, in this household, so much was wrong? No one ever faced the real truth. The life and times of the Wagger family left much to be desired — so much was missing! Love, caring, sharing, honesty. The only common denominator was fear!

I could not find one shred of normalcy lying between the walls of this home. Their home only consisted of breathing objects, facing a lifetime of pain that was felt with each breath. Who would ever have guessed Walter Wagger's last breath would come so soon?

CHAPTER 20

She approached the witness stand, a very attractive lady wearing sophisticated clothing, carrying herself in an extremely professional manner! For the most part, her face was hidden, well beneath the dark glasses she wore, not as an accessory, she explained, but to protect her eyes from the light, which could hinder the healing of a recent eye ailment. Aileen Garnet had been called by the defense to conduct an evaluation on Patricia about three months after the shooting had occurred. She described her first evaluation.

"I first met with Mrs. Wagger on May 31, 1987, while she was lodged in the Upland County Jail. I spent approximately two hours with her and performed an individual counseling consultation with her. During this time, she possessed concerns, fear, and anxiety. She cried and was very restless, jittery, and constantly wringing her hands."

A trait Megan had apparently inherited!

"In my notes, I described Mrs. Wagger as Psycho Motor, which is a term used to describe one's characteristics. There were times when Mrs. Wagger did not appear to be angry, and she denied the death of her husband. She was concerned that he was going to come back to kill her and the children. When we discussed all the things he had done to her, she became angry. I am basing this testimony on my observation and on what Patricia told me. I do not feel she tried, nor did she, manipulate me in any fashion."

Prosecutor Marks was interested in obtaining more details on the first visit, when Mrs. Garnet stated that Patricia denied the death of her husband.

"She denied Walter was dead, and the fear of him was still very strong."

"Mrs. Garnet, do you believe that after all the news coverage and the fact she was lodged in jail, Mrs. Wagger believed her husband was still alive?"

"I believe that is what she was afraid of."

"Is this a normal reaction to this type of situation?"

"I am not qualified to comment on that, as this was my first evaluation of this magnitude."

"Mrs. Garnet, in direct testimony, you never mentioned whether or not Mrs. Wagger showed remorse."

"She was in denial! She had not accepted the fact he was dead. She was angry over the situation regarding the abuse to her and the children, but no, she showed no remorse."

"Over how long of a period did you conduct your evaluation?"

"I completed three between May 31 and July 3, 1987."

This must have been the time frame when Patricia was still in shock. Things had not gone as she had planned. No one was supposed to go to jail! Walter was not supposed to die! The pain was just supposed to end!

I guessed it was easier to deny Walter's death than it was to accept it or take responsibility for it. I would imagine that being lodged in a jail cell would give Patricia plenty of time to think, to try to find another solution to the problem, maybe even discover a route she never considered before. It might even give her the chance to think about waiting until she could have done it herself! God knew there had been plenty of times when it could have been regarded as self-defense. I wasn't condoning the killing of another human being, but at the same time, I was not insinuating that any one person deserved to be beaten on and cursed at everyday of his or her life, especially when it came to the children!

I still could not get past the many cries for help! Or the fact that Walter did not ask for Patricia or his children when, according to witnesses, he knew he was dying. The verbal abuse no longer existed, the physical pain had ended, and so had the life of Walter Wagger! Patricia would pay for the crime she was responsible for being committed, but, on Earth, Walter would never pay for his!

CHAPTER 21

Once again, the spectators, including myself, were becoming quite restless, some to the point that they moved impatiently in their seats, but were too afraid of losing them to leave! Some made frequent trips outside, not caring if there was no place to sit when they returned.

It was a gorgeous day! The sun was shining brightly, and, to tell the truth, I would have much rather been lying in the sun. I continued to tell myself I was here because it was my job, but deep down, I knew it was so much more.

Roberto Solene had been friends with Walter "for a lifetime" and had known Patricia "about ten, maybe fifteen years," having met her shortly after she met Walter the first time. His testimony did not portray a picture of the perfect family — not even close.

"Walter did like to drink! I guess you could say I was his favorite drinking buddy. He had a temper, and when he was drinking his temper flared! Sometimes when nothing and no one brought it on! I remember one night we were out and had stopped at a gas station. I went inside to buy some beer, and when I came out and got back in the car, Walter pulled a pistol on me. He was really mad, and out of nowhere, he asked me if I was sleeping with his wife. I told him no, and finally he calmed down. For a few minutes, I thought he was going to shoot me. On numerous occasions, I had seen Patricia with bruises on her. I knew my friend — I didn't have to ask where she had gotten them."

In cross-examination, Mr. Marks asked Roberto to explain just how good of a friend he was to Walter and Patricia.

"I dated Patricia before she and Walter struck up an affair for the second time. Yes, after they were married, I had sex with Patricia. But Walter knew about me and her having sex."

"Would you like to explain that to the jury?"

"Well, I guess I don't have a choice! On two separate occasions, me and old Walter exchanged partners: it was me and Patricia; Walter and my wife, Gertrude. The one time we were all in the same bed. He knew about it alright, but he sure as hell never got mad."

"Did you ever know of any other men Mrs. Wagger was with?"

"No, Sir. Just me and her husband! If she had been with any other men, I would have known about it. Walter would not have had to ask, he would have known, too."

As Roberto was leaving the witness stand, I could not help but dwell on the old cliché: "Oh what a tangled web we weave."

This marriage was certainly tangled and screwed up. Marriage and a family meant something totally different to me — it meant love, sharing, caring, honesty, and most of all faithfulness. It seemed as though the only sharing that took place in this marriage occurred in the bedroom. It was fine for Patricia to engage in sex with another man, but only if Walter was participating or standing by watching. Everything was on Walter's terms!

It was difficult to comprehend how this couple had survived this long. It certainly appeared as though what this marriage did lack was irrevocable. A decision the two had made nine years ago without thinking of the consequences. I was sure there was love, but not as I knew it!

We had listened to testimony by children, psychiatrists, counselors, law officials, and friends. Who was left?

Her mother!

Seventy-six-year-old Evelyn Billingston, mother of five, had been a widow for close to eight years. She had stood beside her daughter, Patricia, through a teenage pregnancy out of wedlock and an affair with a married man, had raised Patricia's daughter, and had watched and listened as Patricia suffered the abuse.

In 1986, she, too, became a victim of that abuse. Defense Attorney Ray began to speak in a very loud voice, often yelling, which was out of the ordinary for this normally soft-spoken man.

"Mrs. Billingston, can you hear me?"

"Yes!"

"Why is it necessary for me to speak so loudly?"

"Cause I can't hear you if you don't!"

"But why can't you hear me?"

"Because on the weekend before Walter was shot, he hit me in the right ear and busted my ear drum. I haven't been able to hear out of it since."

Testimony had proved one thing about Walter: he was certainly no respecter of persons! When that abuse demon struck, he took his anger out on anybody who was in his way.

"Do you ever recall a time when Walter threatened to kill his wife and kids?"

"Oh, yes! Lots of times! One day that I clearly remember was when Patricia and Walter were living just down the road from us in Greenberg. Patricia asked me to go down to the house with her to visit. When we got there, at first, Walter wouldn't let her in the house. Then he finally let us in and shoved Patricia into the bedroom. He shoved her down on the bed and started beating on her. I tried to stop him, but he told me to get out or I was going to be next. Well, I knew right then he was crazy, so I went outside and sat in the car." She must have been terrified — sitting outside in a vehicle with no help in sight; listening to the sounds of her daughter inside screaming for help as she was getting the hell beat out of her, wondering if she would make it out alive!

"What happened next?"

"Well, they finally came out, and Walter was carrying a gun. He took the keys out of the jeep and told Patricia to get in. So she got in! He held us hostage in that jeep for more than two hours. Patricia was bleeding! He wouldn't even let her have a towel to wipe the blood off her."

"Mrs. Billingston, tell us what happened on the weekend of the shooting."

"Walter came home Saturday, and he was mad as always. Mad because he said Patricia was making him miss work. He just yelled and called us names the first day or so. On Monday, he picked up a butcher knife and said he was going to kill Patricia. He said he was going to line the kids up and make them watch as he cut her head off. Then he said he would kill them, then kill himself. Walter was just a mean man! He was never nice to Megan and was just as mean to Colin. I seen him whip them many a time with a belt, limb, or broom handle. Most of the time, they hadn't done nothing."

My knees were weak, my heart pounding! This man was not only violent, he was demented!

"Mrs. Billingston, how do you feel about your daughter?"

"I love my daughter! I'm not sorry Walter is dead! I never thought about killing him myself, but I knew sooner or later somebody was going to kill him."

"And how do you feel about Megan?"

She began to cry. A brief silence filled the courtroom. I could see that pain she had been trying so hard to hide.

"I love Megan! She is more like a daughter to me than a granddaughter. Me and her have been through a lot together. Megan did what she had to do! It was either Walter or one of them."

This was the first time I had heard anyone use the words "love," "Patricia," and "Megan" with such conviction. She had to wonder where it all went wrong.

Evelyn had just completed the easy portion of her testimony.

The first part of cross-examination involved the letters that had been brought forth earlier in the trial — the ones Delores had not turned over to the prosecution. Mr. Marks asked Mrs. Billingston if she could read the letters.

"No, I can't read them. My eyes aren't as good as they used to be."

Prosecutor Marks then asked for permission to read the letters to find out if Mrs. Billingston remembered receiving them from her daughter while she was lodged in jail. The request was granted.

"'Mom, I hate this place! There has got to be somebody who can get me out of here. Somebody who cares enough! My lawyer says it's up to Megan's testimony whether or not they find me guilty. Mom, if you get the chance to see Megan again by yourself, ask her to do me a favor and not tell anyone I put her up to shooting Walter. Make sure there ain't no Welfare people around when you talk to her. If Megan tells them I put her up to shooting Walter, then I'm as good as gone. I didn't put her up to doing nothing. Ask Megan if she told anybody that I did. Tell her to tell them the truth. That I didn't put her up to shooting Walter! She ain't the one going to prison Mom, it will be me! I love you, Mom! Please don't give up on getting me out of here."

"Mrs. Billingston, do you remember getting this letter from Patricia?"

"Yes, I got that one!"

We were almost back to square one. The letter was read so quickly, one could barely concentrate on each word. Was Patricia trying to get the facts straight or just out to save herself? Who would have ever thought a letter written to her mother in private would wind up being read aloud to a courtroom full of people, being held against you in a court of law! I knew nothing was sacred; the prosecution was leaving no stone unturned. Even the most minor piece of evidence could be just what the jury was looking for.

"Mrs. Billingston, did you ever see Patricia with Wade Bradsworth?"

"No, indeed, I did not! Not with him or any other man other than Walter."

"What about the time Patricia left her husband and went to Wheeler County?"

"When she went down there, she did not leave Walter. I own a trailer down there, and she took me home."

"Did you really see Walter abuse his family?"

"All the time! It was beating, calling names, you name it, and I seen it with my own eyes. I wasn't allowed to spend much time with them until 1986, when Megan and I went to live with them in Appleton. I didn't like what I saw, but I wanted to be with my daughter and the kids."

I felt an astounding surge of sympathy for this woman. She appeared somewhat confused at times, but she managed to hold her own with the man to which so many had fallen prey. So much had happened between she and Patricia, I shivered at the thought of where she would go now. What would happen to her if Patricia went to prison? In many ways, the hell for this family was just beginning.

The courtroom began to empty and court was recessed until Monday morning at 9:00. My eyes stared forward as I watched her being ushered out by the bailiff. I wanted to walk up to her and ask how she was feeling at this time, you know, the typical reporter's question. A question I always looked at with the same answer: How do you think I feel? But this was reality! The case of Patricia Jane Wagger was happening right before my eyes, and unlike television, I was not going to find a happy ending in two hours.

I was well ready for my quiet Sunday at home! I had not known quiet time since this all began. I reminded myself I was here by choice. Patricia was here for responsibility, and Megan was here because she pulled the trigger.

I woke up wondering how they were doing. Did the children attend church with Brother Claude and Miss Jane? Were the children spending time together at all?

Just like every other Sunday of the year, I went to see my mother. The Wagger family was unable to do that. Patricia could not visit her mother on a whim. Mrs. Billingston and the children could not visit Patricia without restrictions. I was deeply saddened by this tragedy. This was no longer a family, only people with the same blood running through their veins.

I prayed those children were no longer in an abusive situation. I prayed that someday, if not now, they would each find the love everyone deserves.

It was a long day, and I knew when Monday rolled around, Patricia would appear in the courtroom ready to tell her side. What was left? In one year, she had lost her husband, her children, her mother, and her friends! Her self-confidence and self-esteem were long gone. As Patricia sat lodged in the county jail, her life was passing before her eyes. As I lie awake, I pondered the many nights they had lay in bed, too afraid to sleep. Fear if any one of them would awake.

I prayed that on this night, they were sleeping fearlessly.

CHAPTER 22

I was awakened Monday morning by the sound of a bird singing outside my window. For a moment, that sound made me forget about work, the trial, the family. Within a couple of hours, I would once again be faced with the suffering they had gone through. It had become such a habit! My mind and body headed for the courthouse without so much as a second thought.

I felt a certain rush of cold chills run down my spine as the defense called its first witness of the day.

"Your Honor, we call the defendant, Patricia Jane Wagger."

It was what I had waited for but was nowhere near prepared to hear.

There she stood with her right hand held at shoulder height. She swore to tell the truth, the whole truth, and nothing but the truth. Each day she had appeared in the courtroom, dressed in a different outfit. None were stylish, but today she wore her best — a blue denim skirt and a pink knit shirt. She was well groomed; her hair clean and styled but certainly not done by a professional. Her clothes were neat but nowhere near fashionable. She was the perfect portrait of a "Plain Jane." She carried herself in a manner that made her very presentable. For six days, I had watched her, but for the first time, I was really seeing her! In a split second, I could see her face and would soon be hearing her voice.

Today was the beginning. In just a short period of time, I would come to feel as though I had known this woman a lifetime. She began by stating her name.

"Patricia Jane Wagger."

"How old are you?"

"Twenty-nine."

"At what address do you reside?"

"I've been residing in Clintsburg for the past nine months since my release from the Upland County Jail, waiting for my trial."

"On what date and where were you born?"

"September 18, 1958, in Lanton County!"

"Who are your parents, and are they still living?"

"Evelyn and Martin Billingston. Mom is still alive. Daddy died in February 1981."

There was that dreaded month again! It seemed as if everything bad happened in February. Coincidence? Perhaps.

"Patricia, tell us about your education."

"I graduated from the eighth grade at Hintersville in Reighton County. I returned to school to finish when Megan was about a year old, but I never graduated."

"What about your home life?"

"Well, growing up was great! I was a spoiled brat! I was the only child Mommy and Daddy had together. I have four half brothers and sisters, but, to tell you the truth, they weren't around much. I got pregnant at sixteen and gave birth to a girl, Megan, when I was seventeen, but I never married her father."

"When did you first meet Walter Wagger?"

"It was either in June or July 1972, at a church social at Lanton. He was sixteen, and I was fifteen. We dated for about two months, then, for some reason, we just broke up."

"Do you know where Walter went after the relationship between you two ended?"

"Yes. He stayed in Lanton, and in 1974, he was married to Charlene Pringle. See, when I was in the hospital giving birth to Megan, she was in the hospital giving birth to their first child. That was October 23, 1975. Then about a year later, I started seeing Walter again."

"Was he still married to Charlene?"

"Yes, but they were having problems."

"How did your relationship with Walter begin the second time?"

"He called me one Sunday evening and asked me out. At first, I said no cause he was married. Then he said it didn't make no difference cause she didn't care or love him anymore, so I said okay. I continued to see him. We developed a sexual relationship, but it was outside Mommy and Daddy's house. See, Daddy said if we were going to do that, it was going to be outside his house. Walter stayed at our house a lot, but we never slept together in the house."

"Was he still married to Charlene?"

"Yes. He stayed part time at my house and part time at their house. It was a real weird relationship, but Walter said he was only staying there so he could see the kids. Then in July 1977, Charlene filed for divorce. During the divorce, our son, Colin, was conceived. He was born in August 1978."

"How did Walter and your father get along with each other?"

"Daddy didn't like Walter. He said he didn't trust him. But I loved him, and Daddy said I had to make up my own mind. He never made me stop seeing him."

"Did you and Walter get married after the divorce?"

"Well, not for a while after it. After Colin was born, me, Walter, and Colin moved to Painstown, when Walter was transferred there with PW Drilling. Then in 1979, me and Walter got married. Right after that, we moved back to Mom's and lived there for a while. Mom didn't like Walter because of the way he did, and Daddy was starting to like him less so we moved to Ashburn."

"Where was Megan during this time?"

"Walter didn't like Megan! When she wasn't with Mom and Daddy, he treated her bad! As long as she was around them, he treated her good. So, me and Mom talked about it and she said they would keep Megan."

"What happened after you moved to Ashburn?"

"Walter left me and went to live with his mother after we had a fight. I moved to Fayestown and tried to live on my own with just Colin, but I couldn't. So I moved back in with Mom and Daddy. A couple of days later, Annie Shepard and I were driving around and saw Walter. Walter stopped and Annie stopped. Walter got out of his truck, came over to Annie's car, and hit her through the window. He started cussing her and asking me why I was running around with such a whore. I jumped out of the car and ran into Annie's sister Emily's house, just across the road where Colin was. Walter came down there and said he wanted to talk and see Colin. He drove me and Colin back to Mom's. We talked for a while, then he went back to Painstown. A couple of days later, he came back to see Colin. This went on for about three weeks, then Walter got an apartment in Painstown, and me and Colin moved down there with him."

"What made you go back to Walter?"

"He asked me, and I said okay cause I loved him. He said he wouldn't beat me up or call me bad names."

"Had Walter done this to you before?"

"Yes! The first time was when I was carrying Colin. I was talking about having an abortion. I mean, we weren't married, and I already had one child. I couldn't take care of her by myself, so I knew I wasn't able to take care of another. Anyway, Walter got mad and pushed me out the door of the trailer we were at. I fell on the ground. The baby wasn't hurt, and I just had some minor bruises from the fall. I decided then that it was best to keep the baby."

"Was this the last time Walter abused you?"

"No! God, no! One time he was talking on the phone to Charlene. This was while we were living with Mom and Daddy. He had been on the phone for over two hours, and it was long distance. I told him to cut the call short, and he got mad. He told me it was none of my Goddamn business who he talked to and for how long. He could talk as long as he wanted. He slammed down the phone and then slapped me across the back with his open hand. I wasn't mad cause he was talking to her, it was just that we didn't have much money, and it wasn't even our phone."

"Was Walter always mean to you?"

"No! He could be nice when he wanted to, but that wasn't very often."

"Was he capable of being gentle?"

"Yeah! Sometimes he would..." Tears began to fill her eyes as she wept openly, attempting to finish the sentence. Sadness filled my heart! I again felt that lump in my throat that was becoming synonymous with anyone who spoke of this life. She apparently was a woman who longed for love. She required it, but received so little. She pulled herself together and continued.

"Sometimes he would hug me and kiss me. He would get me flowers and cards for my birthday. Sometimes he would buy me candy on Valentine's Day."

"How did you feel toward Walter when he was gentle?"

"I loved him, and I wanted him to stay that way."

Those brief moments of affection must have meant more to her than life itself. In testimony prior to Patricia's, I kept asking myself the same question repeatedly: Why did she stay?

Her love for Walter was real, and sometimes it must have taken more guts to stay than to walk away from the only love of a man she had ever known.

"Was it always this way with Walter?"

"No! After we got married, the abuse got worse. He drank more, and the beatings came more often. It seemed like I did all I could to please him and make him happy, but the more I did, the madder he got at me."

"Did Walter ever fire a gun at you?"

"Yes! When I took the jeep and went to visit Mom and Daddy. Mom went back to the house with me, and when we got there, he wouldn't let us in the house. He finally did. Then he started beating me and said he would teach me to leave him. He then took the keys to the jeep for over two hours while he stood outside holding the gun. He fired the gun in the air as I was running to the jeep. Mom was already in it cause Walter wouldn't let her stay in the house. He said I had sold his gun and truck. He had not been drinking, and he said to me and Mom, 'Just make one move and give me a reason to blow both of your heads off.' Walter just seemed to quarrel about everything."

I felt she really had made a concerted effort to love this man. To no avail! There must have been some good times, something that made her forget the beatings and try again, something that made her love him enough to stay.

She proceeded to talk about the many moves the family had made during its nine years together. Most of the time they were on welfare. There was only one place that became home to Patricia after her father died — Cove Corner, where they managed to dwell for over two years. While living there, Patricia gave birth to Michelle in 1984. This brought us to the line of questioning which would tell us more about the abuse.

"I decided to go to class and get my GED. On the second night of class, Walter came to pick me up. He saw men in the class so he never let me go back. I went to work for a man by the name of James Shomaker, but Walter made me quit. He tried to get on there, but they wouldn't hire him, so he said I wasn't going back. He said I had hurt his pride, and I wasn't going to humiliate him anymore. So I quit! About two months later, I went to work for Major Plastics. I worked there for about a year, then I got laid off, and I never went back."

She had only been on the stand for a brief period, and already she was giving us a different view of Walter. He had been a wonderful man to many on the outside, but to his wife and kids, he was a different person. When the term "sexual abuse" came to light, it was far worse than I had imagined. Far worse than being forced to perform sexual intercourse, as if that wasn't enough!

"About four years after we were married, I began to notice a change. He was still beating on me, but he started making me do things I didn't want to do."

"Like what?"

"Like going to bed with other women!"

Oh, God! The faces in the courtroom told the story. Sighs of sickening amazement rang out in the tone of disbelief. Judge Kimble used his authority to silence the sounds.

"When we lived in Greenberg, my niece's picture, along with my name, showed up in a magazine. In a short while, I started getting all these letters from people asking me and Walter to come and visit them. I didn't know why I was getting them for a long time. My niece finally told me her boyfriend did it as a joke. Anyway, there was this one letter from a couple in Chicago, Adam and Blair Tate. Walter liked their letter and told me to answer, so I did. Then we started writing on a regular basis to each other. When we moved to Cove Corner, we continued to write to each other. In one letter, they wanted us to come and see them, but we didn't go. Later on, Walter said to invite them to our house. I didn't want them to come, but Walter did, so finally I agreed. At first, we just went out to dinner and stuff like that. I was a little shocked that Walter didn't get mad. He really didn't like black people, and when they arrived, Blair was black and Adam was white. But it didn't seem to bother Walter, and I didn't mind either. Adam was about fifty or so, and real short. Blair was twenty-nine and real tall. Mainly, we just sat and talked. Then they started wanting to fool around and take pictures. I told Walter I didn't want to do it! He told me I better do it and better act like I liked it, or I would pay for it when they left."

I was certain Patricia did not have to ask Walter to explain such a statement. She knew exactly what he meant. I found her testimony so intriguing, yet so complicated, almost to the point that it was unbelievable. But there was no time to think between sentences.

"It was just me and Blair! We had oral sex while Walter and Adam watched and took pictures."

For a moment, I found it difficult to understand what could have caused such madness. Not that I was a stick in the mud — I firmly believed "to each his own." I would never understand the "forcing" sex. The difficultly lay in understanding how these grown men could get off by just watching and taking pictures, without getting involved. Just watching these women, their wives, engage in sexual activity.

"Patricia, what kind of feelings did you have after you performed these sexual activities?"

"Bad! Dirty! Cheap! Like a whore!"

"Were there other types of sexual abuse during your marriage to Walter?"

"Yes!" she answered, trying to regain her composure.

This could not have been comfortable! Knowing damn well all eyes were staring at her, judging her, not the dead man who had forced her. The exposure of such stories of her participation in these "unusual sexual acts" certainly was not in her favor. This was a small town! Towns surrounding this one were small. If someone's dirty linen was aired, he or she was automatically tainted.

Despite the intricate situation she was in now, this was a consequential component of the abuse she had endured. If she had a chance for acquittal, this was it!

"Walter would always ask me, when we were in bed together, if he was big enough — if he satisfied me, and if it was enough! Sometimes he was gentle when we were making love, but most of the time he was real rough. One time he brought home this extension, you know, a thing to make a man bigger. I don't know where he got it, but he decided to use it. He would make me get into positions like on my hands and knees, then he would ram hisself in me, real hard, while he was wearing that extension! Then he would pull me back real hard! He had it the entire time we were married. He'd use it a couple of times a week. I begged him not to use it, cause it hurt. I told him I didn't like it, but he didn't care. Sometimes, I would pretend to be asleep, but Walter would grab me by the hair and tell me to get up, and then he would use that extension."

Her voice quivered. At times, she could barely speak at all. She hung her head low, as a child being punished for being bad. Looking at this through her eyes, it must have seemed like punishment! To me, it didn't matter what prompted his sexual excitement. The point was she was doing it against her will. Wasn't that a crime within itself? Only if it was reported!

Defense Attorney Ray, in his soft-spoken voice, asked her to continue.

My, God! There is more? More than I could imagine.

"When we lived in Greenberg, Walter got this German Shepherd dog. He kept the dog outside for about a week. Then one day, he brought it inside. He told me to go into the bedroom and take off my clothes. He was being real kind — I thought he was going to make love to me! Then he brought the dog into the bedroom and told me to lay down in the floor; he wanted to see what it was like between a dog and a woman."

Never a dull moment with good ole Walter! That was it! If he hadn't already been dead, I would have wanted to kill him myself. I believed Patricia was telling the truth. Not even the most vivid imagination could dream up such a psychotic action, especially when it was going to make her look worse than she already did! My stomach began to churn, and for a moment, I thought I was going to be sick! Sex with animals had always been quite a joke among younger children, but it was never discussed with an adult! It was sickening to the middle-aged, and non-existent to the older folk. Certainly never an admittance of a turn on! No one actually thought it existed — not in our little town. What an education we were receiving from the plight of Patricia Jane Wagger!

"I begged him not to make me do it! He told me that, if I wanted to live to raise my kids, I would do it. So, I laid down on the floor. Walter stimulated the dog, then positioned it. He just stood back and laughed while the dog had sex with me. After the dog was finished, Walter would make love to me. He wouldn't let me go to the bathroom, take a shower, or nothing. This occurred two or three times a week for about four months. Finally, Walter got rid of the dog."

She wept hard, pausing between words. He forced her to participate in these lewd acts, and she called it "making love."

The courtroom echoed with sounds of... well, I'm not sure! Disbelief, sadness, sympathy, or just plain mortification!

Judge Kimble called for a ten-minute recess.

I knew the defendant was not the only one who needed a break. Many of us gathered in the hallway to smoke cigarettes. As several people held discussions about the things they had just heard, I stood back and listened. Some were making light of it: "My God, she is a dog lover." Many could not believe their ears. Others refused to believe it, while one woman said she wondered why Patricia had not pulled the trigger a long time ago. A young girl standing off to the side said it best when she remarked, "Just be glad it wasn't you." She was looking puzzled at a loud, boisterous man who was making suggestive statements. She spoke in a very peaceful voice, which seemed to shut him up instantly. Again, wisdom from the mouths of babes!

I was trembling at the thought of any human being forcibly contributing to these acts. I remembered thinking, as Patricia was testifying, that she was not an educated woman, but sexually, she had done it all. This recess must have been the shortest one in history.

When court reconvened, Patricia was sitting in the same position as when we had recessed. Her eyes were swollen. In spite of all she had already gone through, she was able to continue in her testimony.

"Patricia, were there other times when Walter sexually abused you?"

"I guess you would call it that. One time, when we lived at Haughton, Walter brought home this guy, Ernie Moreland, who worked with him. Walter told me to send the kids to the neighbors for a little while. After they left, he told me to go into the bedroom and put on my black nightgown. I asked him why. He told me to shut up and just do it! That night, Walter and Ernie both had sex with me."

There it was! At the age of twenty-nine, there was nothing left for her to experience sexually! My mind went back to the testimony of the counselor who stated that, when women suffer from abuse, they do whatever they can to please their abuser. An attempt to keep the beatings from happening. I wasn't yet sold on the fact that Walter was the only one who enjoyed some of the sexual activity, but I had no doubt he was the force behind it. He most unquestionably did not discourage it, yet he beat her when he thought she was taking part in any sexual activity under her own free will. Was that another means of his control? Most of Walter's idea of pleasure Patricia spoke of with great repugnance!

Walter had acted out his most intimate fantasies at the expense of his wife. But they called it love.

Mr. Marks was going to bury her with the information the defense had revealed in an effort to prove what kind of man Walter Wagger was. But deep down, I knew the prosecution already had known it all.

"Patricia, you were practicing birth control the past several years. How did you come to get pregnant with Michael?"

"Walter took the IUD out of me hisself!"

As she began to cry, I began to feel the tears forming in my eyes as well. Shake it off! Here we go again! Was there any part of this woman's private life that was not going to be exposed to the public? Was there any immoral crime this man had not committed toward his wife?

"Please repeat your answer!"

"Walter took the IUD out of me hisself. We were in bed together. He said he wanted another child. He wouldn't let me go to the doctor to have it removed. I had my legs as wide as they would go! He ran his hand up inside me and took it out. It was very painful! I bled quite a bit. Within a couple of weeks, I knew I was pregnant!"

Patricia didn't seem to need a recess now, as the worst part was apparently over, but I kept silently asking the judge to take one. I needed the time to crawl into a corner and be alone!

This was like watching a soap opera, one only shown on a cable channel and only late at night! However, when this segment was over, Patricia was not going to return to her family. There was no happy ending. She was not going home to a fancy house by the ocean. This was real! She was going to return to this real set until the real jury voted on what to do with her.

By now, I was totally addicted to the scene. I could barely wait for the next episode, yet I wanted desperately to break free. But I knew this time I couldn't walk away — no one was going to occupy my time and take my mind off this. Each time I looked at her, her face became more tangled in a web of pain. Each time I focused on Megan, Colin, Michelle, and Michael, I became angry.

Walter had abused the children he already had, and yet he wanted to bring another one into the travesty.

Patricia's voice became more innocent. Each time she cried, the tears fell more rapidly. Her entire married life to Walter was a nightmare! The abuse started even before he married her. Now, more than a year after his death, she was reliving the nightmare all over again. The difference this time was that it was not in private.

My heart went out to her, but I still believed that somehow, somewhere, at sometime, there must have been some good in their relationship. There must have been something that made her fall in love with this man. There must have been something, other than fear, that made her stay. This man was now being portrayed as nothing less than a monster. She had taken part in his sexual activities because she loved him. She had left and gone back because she loved him. She bore his children and gave up her first born because she loved him. Why did she love him?

"Patricia, a letter has been submitted into state's evidence. I ask you to look at this letter and tell me if you recognize it."

"Yes."

"Did you write this letter?"

"Yes, to Mom and Megan."

"Would you read this letter for the court, please?"

"I wrote it on October 27, 1985. 'Dear Mom and Megan, I wish I could have stayed with you when I came down to visit. I wish Steve would come and get me. He's the only one I really love! It's not Walt! The gas company will be here Thursday to shut off the gas because I haven't had the money to pay the bill. I can't even afford to pay attention, much less anything else. Walter bloodied Colin's nose this morning, and no bigger than he is! Mom, could you send me some rat poisoning or liquid rat poison or the money to buy some? If you get it, send it to me. Love, Patricia!'"

"Patricia, who was Steve?"

"Just a guy I met when he was nineteen and I was fourteen!"

"Was he Megan's father?"

"No."

"What brought on the bloody nose?"

"Colin had a remote control jeep, and he broke it. He asked Walter to fix it. Walter couldn't get it fixed. He got mad, blamed Colin, and hit him in the nose with his fist."

"Why did you ask for the rat poison?"

"If I could have got some, I would have killed Walter! I loved him all the time, but it was some of the things he did that I hated!"

"I'm going to hand you another letter and ask you if you wrote this one. If so, will you read it aloud to the court?"

"Yes. 'If I just had one measly shell for that pistol, I would shoot him. That man is so mean. It's a wonder the devil doesn't come right out of the ground and get him. He is so much like his dad, and sometimes I could just choke him. I hate this place, and someday, I'm going to get out of here. I wrote two bad checks just to get some food for Michelle. Mom, please send me some money so I can cover them. I'm scared the Welfare Department is going to come and take the kids from me. They can have Colin but not my little Michelle. She reminds me so much of Megan! I better go before Walt catches me. I don't want to get slapped anymore. My arms are so sore, I can hardly make a cup of coffee. Love, Patricia!'"

"When did you write this letter?"

"I wrote it to Mom and Megan when we were living in Appleton."

"Did you hate Colin?"

"No! I was just angry with him. He had started hitting to get his way. I always got over my anger toward him."

The year 1985 emerged into a breaking point in the marriage of Patricia and Walter. How many times, when people are angry, do they use the phrase "I could just choke you?" Did she ever think those words, in this particular letter, would come back to haunt her? Would be used against her? Would be the words standing between her and prison?

She stated they had been evicted from their home several times because the rent wasn't paid. Yet, prior witnesses had testified to Walter being a good provider. He had blackened her eyes and sent her walking in the rain late at night, but he always came to get her. She always came back. She filed for divorce December 1980, and dropped it. He had done the same on two separate occasions. When things got tough, Walter moved the family to a new location. This was the one time nobody could run. There was no place to hide. What did the last two years of their life together have in store?

"Going back to the first letter you read, when you said you wished you could have stayed down there, what were you referring to?"

"In October 1985, I took the kids and David Vincent down to visit Mom in Wheeler County. He was the only man I had an affair with. I had no intentions of coming back. I really liked David! He was good to me and the kids! He would play ball with them and read to them, stuff like that. He was really nice! He didn't treat me like Walter did. I knew him about two weeks before we left. We had a physical relationship for about a week or two. Then Walter came down and took Colin and Michelle. Walter filed for divorce, saying I had abandoned the kids. He kept calling me down at Mom's cause I was going to stay and fight for my kids! The last time he called, he said if I ever wanted to see my kids alive again, I better get back that day. So, I came home! That ended my relationship with David."

"Patricia, what kind of man was Walter to the kids?"

"Well, he always called Megan a red-headed bitch and told her we found her under a garbage can. When we lived at Appleton, Colin got a can of potted meat out of the cabinet, took one bite out of it, and threw it away because he didn't like it. I asked who had done it. Colin said he didn't do it, and Megan said she didn't do it. This was after Mom and Megan came to live with us. Walter said he would make them tell me the truth about who had done it. First, he went and got a belt. The kids started crying. Then he said he had a way of making them tell the truth. He went and got a rat-trap and let it go off in their faces. Then he set it again, grabbed Megan's hand, and told them he was going to cut off their fingers if they didn't tell him who did it. So, Megan said she did it! Walter let the trap go off, then he whipped Megan with a belt. One time, Colin got a piece of chocolate cake without asking. Walter put black pepper down his throat and some of it got in his eyes. One time, Megan asked me if she could stay with a friend, and I said yes. The kids were never allowed to have friends over at our house while Walter was home. So, when he came home, he wanted to know where Megan was. I told him where she was, and he said when she got home he was going to beat her. So, when she came home, he did!"

I immediately noticed the change in her voice when she began to talk about the abuse to the kids. It was as if a major anger had taken over. Her tone was not that of a sympathetic cry, but one of animosity that she would never forget or forgive! It didn't seem to be a problem with Walter to send the kids to a neighbor while he engaged in his sexual tryst, but if it was something they wanted, it was against the rules. Was he afraid of what they might tell? Or did he simply have a pattern of giving people only what he wanted?

"Patricia, did any of the physical problems ever occur in public?"

"Once. When we lived in Farmtown. Walter got mad at me and tried to drive a motorcycle in the living room. Mom and Megan were in the bedroom. He went into the bedroom and called Mom an old bitch and told her she stunk. He told her he wished he had never seen her or Megan. Then, he came back into the living room and took his belt off. He started beating me because I wouldn't go next door and ask this girl to go to bed with him."

Time after time, sentence after sentence, she spoke of abuse in some fashion. It happened when they were alone. It happened when they were with other people. Those kids saw it, heard it, and were often the object of it. It had just become routine in their lives. Mommy and Daddy fighting — as common to the Wagger children as breathing is to all of us!

He blamed her for it all — from a washing machine falling in the back of a truck to being laid off from his job! His attitude rubbed off on his son at an early age. By the age of nine, Colin was fighting, not only at home, but in school as well, to get his way. What were his chances of being normal?

Shortly after the death of their father, these kids were torn apart! The youngest three went in one direction, with Megan, who had already been tossed around so much, once again on her own. Even separated, it had to be a better life than that to which they had grown accustomed. How was this going to affect them in the long run? Fighting, drinking, cursing, physical abuse — it was all they had known! It was what made a relationship! The blessed one was the youngest, who, by the grace of God, would not remember. I prayed they had all gotten out before it was too late. God love the children!

CHAPTER 23

It had been a difficult seven days. The courtroom was often like a movie. There were moments of laughter, moments of tears, moments of agitation, and hours of disbelief!

Most of the testimony was repetitious. Nevertheless, it was never dull.

Although much had been revealed in this mountain of evidence, there were still rivers of questions to be answered. There were times when I could not imagine her being found guilty and times when I saw no way out. As much as I attempted to cipher it all out, I could not find a conclusive verdict. The jury was fortunate I was not a member. Otherwise, they would have never reached a verdict!

I anticipated an ending, just as I was certain Patricia had done daily for the past year. Each time I looked at her, her eyes poised straight ahead, it was apparent she was pondering the outcome.

Walter Wagger was being termed as the victim, but was he really? For years, he had been tormented by demons – abuse and alcohol! Those demons tormented his family. For Walter, it was over! He was free from those demons. But those demons would live on in his family long after his freedom had been granted.

For a period of time, Walter had not been employed. Then, in January 1987, he became a truck driver — a job that would keep him away from his family. The Wagger family had moved from the Harald Apartments, known as the "anything goes capitol" in Upland County. But they did not go far, only across the street into a small, two-bedroom house on Glendon Road. Patricia, Megan, Colin, Michelle, Michael, and Mrs. Billingston, along with Walter, shared this home. Seven people, two bedrooms. Walter had only been home a couple of times since beginning his newfound profession, so Patricia was left with a lot of leisure time! His absence gave her time to socialize with her friends at the apartments and the opportunity to meet new ones. It was not out of the ordinary for extramarital affairs to take place at the apartments. Nor was it unusual for rumors to fly, even if an affair had never taken place. After all, Mrs. Poole would see to that! It was a reputation one automatically assumed upon becoming a resident. As the witness, Delores, stated, "Everyone slept with everyone at the Harald Apartments."

During one particular social gathering, Patricia met the man who would become the instigator of the worst fight yet between she and Walter. At the very least, it would be their last. James Wade Bradsworth! Not only a familiar name, but also a face that would long remain in my memory. He had come to Appleton from Florida with Mr. Carder's daughter. Well, we had already met Mr. Carder, the one who testified that, after the shooting, he went to bed and attempted to sleep. The others, including the defendant, congregated in his apartment. The phone was ringing, people were talking, yet he knew nothing about the shooting! I figured the man could have slept through an earthquake if he missed all that commotion.

Patricia continued her testimony with an explanation of her encounter with Wade Bradsworth.

"The first time I met him, we were at a party, and Wade was telling my fortune with seashells. The next time, I was at Darlene's apartment, and he came over and asked me for a cigarette. So, I gave him one, then he left. The next time was when he came to my house on February 20, 1987. He came over and asked me if he could borrow the jeep. He said that he had some dishes and stuff to pick up at this woman's house. I told him several times no, but he kept asking. Finally, I told him he could. He brought the jeep back, but he never told me he wrecked it. He brought the keys into the house and said thanks, then left. In just a few minutes, Megan and Colin came into the house and told me the jeep had been wrecked. So, I called the law! They said they would be out, but they never came."

The first unanswered cry for help leading up to that dreadful day!

"Then, I called him, and he said the guys with him were playing around. The jeep went off the road and struck a tree. He said he would call his mother and see if she would send him money to fix it cause he didn't have no insurance. He never came back, and I couldn't find him. I didn't tell Walter until the following Friday because I couldn't get a hold of him. He was on the road, and they told me when he checked in they would have him call me. So, when he called Friday, I told him what had happened, and he said he was coming home."

"Patricia, did you ever have an affair with Wade Bradsworth?"

"No, I did not! He was nothing more than an acquaintance."

So why did she let him borrow the jeep? It was such a task to find a solid answer to any of my questions. What made her do some of the things she had done? Some were under Walter's thumb, some on her own accord. What made her finally snap? It had been a long time coming. Every dog has its day. We reap what we sow. The shooting itself was comprehendible, but the validity of the timing was difficult to consume. Whether one knew the answers or not was basically irrelevant! What would transpire in the Wagger home in the days ahead would be the result of allowing that acquaintance to borrow the jeep.

CHAPTER 24

The week between the accident and Walter's trip home turned out to be the final week of freedom and socializing for Patricia. She knew Walter was mad when she called him about the jeep. She was not surprised to find him equally mad when he arrived home.

"When Walter got home Saturday the first thing he did was look at the jeep. He started screaming at me saying, 'I thought you told me it wasn't tore up that bad!' The more he looked at it, the madder he got. I told him that I had told him how bad the jeep was. He called me a lyin' bitch and said I must have been sleeping with Wade, or I never would have let him drive that jeep. He pushed me toward the house and told me to get in there and stay."

What? No kiss? No hello? No "how are the kids?" That apparently was too much to ask of a man with so much anger over his vehicle. No show of affection for the wife and kids he hadn't seen in two weeks. This time, she had given him a reason to be angry, or at least the closest thing to a reason that we had heard.

"Then, Walter came inside and threatened to beat Colin to death if he didn't tell him what happened. Colin told Walter that Wade Bradsworth had brought back the jeep, and it was wrecked. Then Walter got even madder! I tried to tell him there was nothing between me and Wade, but he wouldn't listen. I knew then that it was going to be a long weekend! I already wanted him to go back on the road. Then, Walter went over to the apartments to find out what was going on while he was away. About thirty minutes later, he came back over to the house and was madder than ever. He said, 'You have slept with that son-of-a-bitch. I know you have! Those people over at the apartments are just lyin' to cover your ass!' This went on all day! Walter finally went to bed and calmed down some. During that time, Walter shoved me and slapped me twice. He said just as soon as he found out what happened, he was going to kill me. At that point, he had not been drinking."

"Did you call the 911 center that night?"

"Yes! Everybody was fighting over at the apartments, so at one time I called. I told them my husband was asleep now but had been beating on me, and I wanted a deputy to call me. I also told them they were fighting next door, and I wanted them to stop them. I was afraid they were going to wake Walter up. He was already mad anyway!"

"Let's go to Sunday. What happened then?"

"I thought Walter would be in a better mood, and we could talk. But he wasn't! I tried to tell him Wade borrowed and wrecked the jeep, but he said he didn't want to hear it from me cause I would just lie anyway. He got up and went back over to the apartments. When he came back over to the house, he started calling me names and hitting me. He pulled my hair and spit in my face. He had not had nothing to drink that I could tell. I hadn't seen him drink nothing, but I could smell a little alcohol on his breath. The disturbance over at the apartments carried over into Sunday as well, finally ending about 5:30 or 6:00 Monday morning. I guess no one really felt like messing with Walter."

Apparently, Sunday was not a day of worship at the Wagger home. Megan had gotten up and gone to church with Brother McMillihen, but no one else attended Sunday services.

The anger Walter was feeling awoke at the same time he got out of bed! Anger he harbored all through the night. During the course of the day, he had pushed Patricia into the bedroom and held a butcher knife to her throat, as had been established during prior testimony. Toward evening, he ripped her shirt and began to choke her with the rest of the shirt. The anger was also geared toward the children.

"Walter said that Michael, only four months old then, didn't deserve a mother like me. I was nothing but a whore. With the knife in his hand, he stood over the baby's bed and said that killing the baby would cause me more pain than killing me. I started crying and begged him not to hurt the baby. He shoved me down on the bed and said he was going to make love to me whether I wanted him to or not. He started pulling on my jeans, trying to get them off. While he had me held down, I scratched him. That made him mad! His arm started bleeding and he said, 'See what you did, bitch? Lick it off!' I wouldn't do it, so he tore off my jeans and made love to me."

There was that phrase again – "making love!" I'm sorry, but from what I

114

was hearing, his performance was nothing more than rape.

"After he did that, he got up and said he was going back to the apartments. He was going to find out what was going on, and this time, somebody was going to tell him. I had tried, but he wouldn't listen. The people at the apartments had tried to tell him, but they weren't telling him what he wanted to hear."

I couldn't help but wonder why she didn't just tell him what he wanted to hear. After all, he was beating her anyway! Maybe if he heard she was having an affair with Wade, he would just leave. Just file for divorce and maybe, this time, carry it out. But that wasn't what happened, and somebody was going to suffer the consequences. For Walter Wagger, there would be no more control over anyone.

"Patricia, who all was at your home Sunday night?"

"Me, Mom, and the kids."

"Did the beatings and name calling continue after Walter came back from the apartments?"

"Yes! Only this time, he started on Mom and Megan. He called Mom an old hag and asked her if she wanted some of what he gave me. Every time he called me a name, he hit me. I was aching all over. I hadn't slept at all! I guess I had no feelings!"

I was able to sympathize with her in the no sleep department, but for totally different reasons. Ever since this trial began, I had carried it home with me. I couldn't close my eyes without seeing that child, crying and begging for the beatings to stop. I tried to envision the nine years of Patricia's life living under this scrutiny. I tried to visualize the weekend before the shooting. The brutality, the pain, the fear, the anger — all of which ended when somebody died! Where did the love come in? She lived this way at the hands of somebody so violent and stayed for the love?

CHAPTER 25

It was time to move on to Monday. We had gone through the lunch recess and a ten-minute recess. As I looked at my watch, I realized the seventh day was about to come to a close.

The last twenty-four hours of Walter's life started when he got out of bed. He headed back to the apartments, still looking for that small fragment of evidence connecting his wife sexually to Wade Bradsworth. The anger had not diminished in three days. If anything, it had increased. Again, before he left the house for his repeated journey, he told her, "If I don't find something out, I'm coming back over here, and I'm killing you."

She believed every word he said. This was not a new phrase that Walter had concocted. He had used it often! So why did those words mean more to her this time? The only way I could describe it was that they had crossed that fine line between love and hate! By then, neither knew which side they were on. Patricia was asked to continue with Monday.

"Walter told me he could not take anymore of me. He said he hated me and he wished I was out of his sight. He came back from the apartments and whipped the kids for not going to school. They had been up till real late because of all the fighting. They were tired, so I told them just to stay home. They had missed the bus anyway and didn't have a way."

If everything I had heard was factual, who the hell felt like going to school? Although, the children were probably better off at school than at home. At least they were safer. At school, they would be spared from hearing, seeing, and feeling the incidents taking place in their home.

"Patricia, who took care of Michael?"

"Megan! She took care of all of them. I couldn't! My arms were so sore that I couldn't even pick him up. Megan did a good job with the kids, but she took care of them all the time. She loved her brothers and sister."

There was never a doubt in my mind that Megan was all a mother could ask for. She had definitely always come to the rescue. She fought with them, but also fought for them — right to the bitter end!

"The kids had seen the abusive events over the past three days. At about 6:30 that evening, Walter came in and said he was going to get a tire for the car. When he came back, he had vodka and orange juice. He had already been drinking. He got on the phone and called his brother. Then he called his ex-wife. He asked them to keep the kids, but they said no. Then, he called his boss and asked for the rest of the week off. He said he had some business to take care of at home. I also heard him ask his boss if his wife knew anyone who could watch the three kids. Then, he fixed him a drink and drank it straight down. He fixed him another and drank it straight down. Then, he fixed the third one and headed over to the Harald Apartments."

What was he up to? Speculation might imply he did intend to kill his wife and maybe himself! Maybe he was just planning to take the three kids and leave. I guess no one will ever know his intentions behind those phone calls.

"Were you over at the apartments Sunday?"

"Well at one time Sunday, Walter took me over to Delores's apartment. He said she told him something about a man I was supposed to be seeing. He said to Delores, 'Now, tell her what you told me about this man, her boyfriend.' Delores wouldn't say anything, so Walter ordered me back to the house, and he stayed over there."

The fear and intimidation were not solely restricted to the Wagger home that weekend. With the many trips he had made to the apartment building, they were pouring out onto the tenants there. This time, so many of them had seen the real Walter Wagger! I began to tremble as the defense directed our attention back to Monday. The end was near!

"At about 9:30, Walter came to get him another drink. I didn't know what he was doing at the apartments, and no one ever told me. When he came back, he started calling me names. He stomped on my foot. He said, 'Bitch, you better be gone when I get back, or so help me God, I will kill you. Get your mother and your daughter and get out of here.' I asked for the car keys but he just ignored me. He fixed his drink, and he left."

She paused for a moment, as if to recompose herself in preparation for the final hours. The time frame seemed pretty accurate between witnesses. I guess in her shoes, had somebody threatened to kill me, I would have watched

117

the clock, too, counting down the hours until what could be my final breath. It would not have been my first choice, but if I planned on staying to fight the odds, I would have kept up with the time. Right then, it was all she had! By then, the two seemed to be trying to outlast the other, trying to determine which one was stronger. Who could hold on longer?

If Patricia had stayed that time, then she had fought back. Walter taught her well. If she had left before he cooled off, and he came to get her, the entire vicious cycle would have started all over again. Did it ever cross either's mind that one might not survive to have another chance?

"At 11:00 or 11:30, Walter came back home. Mommy and the two boys were asleep. Megan and Michelle were in the kitchen fixing something to eat. He came through the door and kicked me. He said, 'Bitch, I thought I told you to be gone.' My body was hurting all over! I was so sore! I had been beaten so much in the past three days that I didn't care if I lived or died. He went into the kitchen and said to Megan, 'Move, you little bastard, redheaded bitch, or I'll knock your head through the wall!' He then told me to get in the kitchen and fix him something to eat. He fixed him a drink, using the last of the vodka and orange juice. Megan said she would fix him something to eat."

There she was again! Megan to the rescue! I became so angry at the thought of this alleged adult, who called himself a man, talking to this child the way he had. The one person who admittedly hated him, yet she permitted him to beat on her and call her names, rather than watch it happen to her brothers and sister. I tried to picture the huge man, how he got his rocks off by beating on others so much smaller than him. Somehow, I felt his size alone could maintain control of his household. He was the "man of the house," but a poor excuse for a man!

I could see the face of Megan as she sat on the witness stand. So small sitting in that chair! Would she ever put this behind her? Would her days with Walter Wagger haunt her long after his body had decayed?

"So, Megan went and fixed him some sauerkraut and wieners. I took them into him and tried to wake him. He just moaned and told me not to touch him. He had gone into the living room and sat down in the chair. Then, Megan took the plate back into the kitchen. Megan and Michelle went into the living room and ate, then they went to bed. I was sitting in the living room. I guess it was about 12:30 or so."

I guess the time was no longer a factor!

"What happened next?"

"I don't really know. I just got the gun from my closet and put it in Mom and

Megan's bedroom. I was going to shoot him if I got the chance! Megan got back up, and I asked her to get the gun for me, so she did. I told her to turn out the light. She asked me if I was going to kill him, and I didn't say nothing. She went back to bed. I wasn't thinking straight! I just wanted him to stop beating me. I hated him for what he did to me, but I didn't hate Walter."

"What happened next?"

"I laid the gun down on the loveseat and went into the kitchen. Then, I went into Megan's bedroom, but I don't know if she was asleep or not. I asked her if she would get up and talk to me, so she did. While we were talking, Megan said if Walter got up, he was going to kill all of us. I told her there was nothing I could do about it. She then asked me where I put the gun. She told me if I wasn't going to kill him, she was. I didn't try to stop her! I didn't care!"

My hands were shaking and my palms were sweating. It was impossible to remember exactly what I was doing in this courtroom. I had dug a hole and buried myself in this family. I was taken back to every incident brought to light throughout the trial: the dog, the black pepper, the rat-trap, the butcher knife, the hostage situation, the name-calling, and the beatings! I could feel the mood that led up to the shooting. Thank God, I was only feeling the aftermath.

Her voice began to quiver as Defense Attorney Ray asked her what happened next.

"Megan went and got the gun. Evidently, it wouldn't fire! She brought it into the kitchen to me. I checked it and sent her back into the living room to try again. She brought the gun in to me three times. I checked it three times and sent her to try again. Then, on the third try, it fired! I don't remember this part real well. Megan came back into the kitchen with the gun. She dropped it on the floor and said, 'There, Mommy, he won't ever hurt us anymore. He's dead.'"

I felt relief! It was if I had known this evil man, and at last, justice was served! I could not possibly know how this family had lived, or how they must be feeling now that it was over. The abuse they had suffered at the hands of Walter Wagger was over. Megan was right! He would never hurt them anymore.

Patricia took a brief moment to regain her composure before continuing with the early morning hours of February 27, 1987.

"I didn't know what to do. She had shot him, and all I could think to do was call 911. So, I called and told them I had shot my husband. I didn't want them to know Megan had done it. I wanted to protect her, just as she was doing for me. I heard a noise like he was getting up — that was when I called 911. I guess the noise brought me back or something. I went over to Roger's apartment and

119

asked him to go over and see if Walter was still alive. I waited for a few minutes, then I went back over to the house. I didn't go into the living room while Walter was there. I never saw Walter again! I stayed in the kitchen and left only when I went outside to talk to Deputy Knicely. When I came back into the house, Walter was already gone. I mean the ambulance had already taken him. I went over to Delores's apartment, and I just stayed there."

"Do you remember someone calling from Minnerstown Medical Center?"

"Yes, the doctor called and said he needed permission to operate on Walter. I told him to go ahead. He said he couldn't without me signing some papers. I couldn't get there. The next time they called, they said Walter had died."

For the first time in hours, she began to cry — uncontrollably! The defense paused for a moment and asked if she needed to take a recess.

"No, I'd like to go on. I don't really remember what I did when they told me Walter had died. I know I ran out of the apartment, but the next thing I remember was sitting on Delores's couch drinking coffee. I went back to my house about 9:30 that morning. Mommy was in the house by herself. The kids had stayed over at Delores's apartment with me. Then the people from the TV station came and wanted to talk to me and the kids. I can't recall the time. I just wanted to get a bath. I hadn't bathed or changed my clothes all weekend. The TV crew was taking pictures of the house. I let them talk to Megan and Colin, but that is about all I remember."

"Why didn't you leave that night?"

"Walter had the keys to both vehicles in his pocket. And there was Mommy, she's an old lady, plus I had a five-month-old baby and three other kids. Where was I going to go?"

"Do you remember asking Megan to shoot Walter?"

"No! But if Megan says I did, then I did. Megan wouldn't lie! I hadn't thought anymore about shooting Walter after I loaded the gun Sunday. Until that night, I hadn't slept for two days. I was exhausted! I don't know what I was thinking. I was more afraid than I had ever been. There was something about this time that made it different from before. I knew somebody was going to die! I knew he was going to kill me when he woke up. He hadn't calmed down since he got home. I didn't shoot him, but it's my fault Walter is dead."

"How do you feel toward Megan?"

"There was a period of time when I couldn't look at her. I couldn't talk to her, but that didn't last long. I love my daughter! I love all my kids! The last thing I wanted was for them to have to go through anymore. They had been through enough! I wanted to leave Walter. I really did! But he told me if I ever left him again, he would hunt me down and kill me. There would be no place on this earth that I would be safe. The times I did leave, he would follow me, take the kids, and then I'd come back."

"When were you sent to jail?"

"February 28, 1987."

This brought us not only to the closing of the defense's questions, but also to the closing of another day. It was a hell of a time to be closing this segment, but it was late. Others had families waiting at home. Tomorrow morning, they would leave those families behind and return once more to this courtroom, thankful for what they had, listening to the life of the less fortunate!

Already, this trial had been long, and it was only half over! The beginning of the next day would make exactly nine days since testimony began. The days depicted the perfect summer in Upland County, but it wasn't as if many of us were getting to enjoy it. I knew Patricia's notice of the season was a quick peek out the window or maybe the sunlight on her face as she was escorted from her jail cell into the courthouse.

This was the first of many summers the family would spend apart. No picnics in the park or swimming at the lake — at least not together.

I thought the defense had come to life in the questioning of Patricia. It managed to bring out facts that were crucial to the end. Unfortunately, among those facts dwelled many impurities.

Chapter 26

It was Tuesday! The prosecution would begin its questioning of Patricia right where the defense had left off. My memory did not need to be refreshed. From the beginning of the trial, testimony had brought about mixed emotions. But Patricia's testimony matched Megan's in magnitude — it was all very clear!

How could Mr. Marks possibly take Patricia's testimony and turn it against her? He did not have an easy job. How did one ever remain unbiased in times like these? I had to remind myself that he had taken the same oath as I: to remain without opinion, at least in the public eye! He had to believe she was guilty for her part in this murder beyond conviction. He could not let the reasoning behind it cloud what had occurred. How could he sit in the prosecutor's chair, listen to the defendant, and then seek, find, and present his case without some prejudice? But he did! That's why he was the prosecutor.

At last, we continued. Prosecutor Marks began his questioning very bluntly.

"Mrs. Wagger, isn't it true that on February 26, 1987, you asked your eleven-year-old daughter three or four times to kill Walter Wagger?"

"I don't remember!"

Her attitude had changed since yesterday's testimony. Yesterday, her voice denoted animosity and sadness; today, it was hostility!

"Didn't you get the rifle out Sunday and load it?"

"Yes. I was going to kill Walter if I got the chance. I intended to kill him the next time he started beating me. But then I put the gun away."

"When was the next time you thought about shooting your husband?"

"After he came home Monday night and sat down in the chair. I hadn't thought about shooting him all day Monday. It was just right when it happened."

"Where did you put the gun after Megan brought it to you?"

"I placed it on the loveseat and covered it up with a coat so he wouldn't see it if he woke up."

"How long did you remain in the room with Walter before the shooting took place?"

"I don't know... somewhere between five and twenty minutes."

"Were you not planning to shoot your husband all the time you were sitting there?"

"It was just a thought. I wasn't planning anything!"

"Isn't it true that you got Megan out of bed and encouraged her to shoot Walter Wagger?"

"I'm not going to admit I encouraged her. I didn't try to stop her. But I didn't get her out of bed for that reason."

"Mrs. Wagger, were you not standing in the kitchen with your hands over your ears in an effort to not hear the gun discharge?"

"I couldn't see her from where I was standing. Yes! I had my hands over my ears, but not so I wouldn't hear the gun."

He was tough. So was she! It was a toss-up to see who was going to outlast the other in sarcasm. For the moment, Mr. Marks seemed to be satisfied that she was answering the questions indirectly. Then again, they had already been answered. So far!

"In your own testimony, you said your daughter came into the kitchen and told you the gun would not fire. What did you do then?"

"I can't recall."

"Mrs. Wagger, didn't you pull back the bolt on the gun and tell your daughter to pull harder?"

This soft-spoken attorney was now beginning to carry a tone of frustration, and immediately, Patricia seemed to notice.

"Okay! Yes, I checked the gun and sent her back into the living room."

"And didn't you do this three times altogether?"

"I don't remember!"

"Wasn't it in your statement to Sheriff Gossett that you sent Megan in three times before the gun fired?"

"If that is what the statement says then that is what I did. Megan thought about killing him as well as me. But I said I was responsible for Walter's death."

I knew what she was attempting to do. Every witness who had been on the stand and defended her before had been manipulated by this prosecutor. By the time each one had left the stand, we were left wondering what to believe. I was under the impression she was not going to let that happen to her.

"Mrs. Wagger, were you still in the kitchen with your hands over your ears on the third try?"

"Yes! But even through my hands, I could hear the gun fire."

"After Megan shot your husband, what did you do with the gun?"

"I picked it up from the floor and placed it on the bar."

"Instead of having your daughter shoot Walter, why didn't you shoot him yourself?"

"I should have been the one who shot him, not Megan. I have been sorry all along that I didn't do it myself."

"And the reason you called 911 was because you heard Walter move, and you were afraid he was still alive. Isn't that true?"

"No! I called 911 because I knew he was hurt, and I wanted an ambulance and the State Police."

"Mrs. Wagger, Deputy Knicely stated you were not nervous the night he questioned you about the shooting, correct?"

"Well, it was morning, and yes, I heard him. I was nervous, but I was also in the back of the cruiser, and he was up front. He just didn't pick up on it."

I wondered how long it was going to take this prosecutor to come to life. So far, he was playing her game. After all, this was the moment for which he had been waiting. Watching shows like this on television, I would automatically assume the characters were mere actors. But this was not television, and no one was acting. With each question came the voice of judgment. With each answer came the voice of sarcasm. Each one was trying to maintain control! The more she spoke, the more sarcastic she became. The more sarcasm she unveiled, the more irritated he became. She was emitting the characteristics of a hostile witness.

"You've heard Deputy Knicely and Sheriff Gossett tell of the fabrications in your statement." He handed her the statement read by Deputy Knicely that she had given at the time of the shooting. He allowed her to read it briefly then asked, "Is this statement true?"

"No, but I was scared! I didn't know what the truth was right then. The paramedics were inside with my husband, and I wasn't thinking straight. I was trying to protect Megan, too."

"Didn't you really give this statement just to save your bacon?"

For the first time the defense objected as the courtroom filled with low sounds of laughter. The prosecutor had been so tense, yet he had remained so professional in his line of questioning. To hear such a statement coming from him really was quite humorous. Judge Kimble, with a half-cocked grin on his face, ordered Mr. Marks to rephrase the question.

"Mrs. Wagger, wasn't the lie just to protect you?"

"No, it was not! I didn't want anything to happen to Megan."

This courtroom was beginning to sound like a verbal war zone, the defendant trying hard to answer each question so as not to incriminate herself and the prosecutor seeking that final breaking point! He was not satisfied with her answers but, for now, was appeased.

"Isn't it true that you told your daughter what to tell the news reporter?"

"I guess I told her a little, but not everything. I told her some things that night, but not after the news reporters came. I told her to tell the officer that I was asleep on the loveseat when she shot Walter. I don't recall telling her to say that, or anything else, to the news reporters."

"Did you tell Sheriff Gossett the truth about what happened?"

"Yes, I did!"

"Mrs. Wagger, you denied having an affair with Wade Bradsworth. So if he was to get on the witness stand and say that you did have an affair with him, he would be lying. Is that correct?"

"Yes! He was nothing more than an acquaintance."

"Then we should believe you? You lied to Deputy Knicely, you lied to the reporters, and you forced your daughter to lie. So why should this court believe you now?"

"Because I am telling the truth!"

Her voice was beginning to raise now. Nobody appreciates being called a liar. Mr. Marks was on the verge of finding that breaking point.

"But testimony has proven that you didn't even tell your husband the truth about the jeep."

This time the question barely made its way out of his mouth before she was responding.

"I told him the truth. But like you, he didn't want to believe me!"

"Wasn't that why Walter was so mad? Because he found out you hadn't told him the truth?"

"No!"

"You testified that your husband said, 'You didn't tell me the jeep was this bad.' Did you not?"

"Yes, but I told him. He was mad because he thought I was having an affair with Wade Bradsworth."

"But you deny having that affair?"

"Yes, I deny it."

"So Mr. Wagger was mad because you were having an affair?"

"Because he thought I was having an affair. And he said I hadn't paid the bills."

There was very little that the prosecutor reworded that she failed to pick up on. Small words, like "having" rather than "thought," which would have made a difference! But she caught on! I was sure, one way or another, she had been warned about the shrewdness of the prosecuting attorney. For the past eight days, she had seen him in action. She was to respect him, but she was not going to fall prey to his antics.

"You said your husband beat you all weekend, and you never left. Isn't it true that he had beaten you on numerous occasions before, and you never left?"

"I left Walter many times, but he always came and got me."

"Were you always forced to come back, or were there times when you came back on your own?"

"I came back on my own sometimes. I loved my husband. I wanted to make my marriage work, if for no other reason than for the kids to stay together!"

"But they are not together now, are they Mrs. Wagger?"

"No! They are not together."

"Monday, when Walter went to town, how long was he gone?"

"I don't know. About three hours I guess."

"So even though he had told you, 'Bitch, you better be gone when I get back,' you stayed there for those three hours?"

"Yes, because he always came after me when I left. Besides, he had both sets of keys. After Walter beat me, he would calm down. I thought that would happen this time, too."

"He didn't really care about you though, did he? He only came to get the kids, not you. Isn't that correct?"

What a horrifying statement to hear. First, she had to relive the last actual name her husband called her — not "honey," not "sweetheart," not even her name — just "bitch!" That really had to do something for her self-esteem. She was referred to as "bitch" in this courtroom on numerous occasions! Now she sat facing the crowd as the prosecutor told her that, after nine years of marriage, her husband really didn't give a damn about her at all. She felt he loved her, and even the strongest man in this courtroom was not going to change her feelings. He loved her, all right — he just had a poor way of expressing that love.

She responded to his question.

"Yes, I suppose! When he was mad, he just cared about the kids. But when Walter was gentle, I know he loved me. He was two different people! The Walter that was abusive didn't give a damn about me, but the Walter who brought me flowers and kissed and hugged me, he loved me!"

"So the times you left and he came to where you were, he was really just coming to get the kids. Isn't that right?"

"No! He always asked me to come back home with him. He told me the beatings would stop. He was gentle and kind! Those were the times I loved him, and those were the times I would come back."

So what made her come back? Was it the promise that it would end? Was it the threat to take the children? Or the love she felt deep inside for him? The good times that somehow outweighed the bad? Unless one is unfortunate enough to be put in that situation, there is no answer. Maybe it was all of the above.

Walter had made so many idle promises, and those were worth no more than the divorce papers he had filed. But in her mind, she loved him. Did she really know what love was? Other than Walter, she had no relationships of which to speak. The crush she had on a nineteen-year-old when she was fourteen, a teenage relationship that produced a child, and a two-week affair during her marriage to Walter! What did she really know about love besides a gut feeling that kept her heart beating in spite of the fear? Everything she knew about love, she had been taught by Walter.

"But all he really wanted from this marriage was his kids!"

"Sometimes, I guess so!"

Her voice was really starting to weaken. She was becoming quite tired, and it was showing in her face. The prosecutor was taking every stab imaginable to convince the jury she was in this marriage because she wanted to be. Leaving no stone unturned, by simply rewording the very questions asked by the defense, he was making her look more like a villain than a victim. But if Walter only loved his kids, why was it that he treated them all the same way? If his behavior was a show of love for the children, then I'm sorry, but he loved Patricia equally as much, if not more.

"Mrs. Wagger, isn't it true that Walter came in about 11:30 Monday night and passed out in the chair? You tried to wake him and knew it was impossible. That is when you began to put your plan into action."

"I didn't have no plan!"

"Didn't you have your daughter to bring your gun to you? Then, after she was in bed and asleep, you got her out of bed to kill your husband?"

"I did have her to bring me the gun. I laid it on the loveseat and covered it up. Yes, I woke Megan up, but not so she could kill my husband, so I could talk to her. Megan had told me several times that she didn't like Walter. She wanted him dead, too! She was tired of Walter beating her and calling her names. We were all tired of it. Somebody was going to die! It was just a matter of when and who."

"And you tried real hard to stop her from committing this murder, didn't you Mrs. Wagger?"

"No, I did not try to stop her."

"So Megan was really just a part of your plan?"

"No! I told you, I did not have a plan. I told Megan the day before that if I got the chance, I was going to kill him. I wanted him dead! I wanted the beatings to stop!"

Prosecutor Marks had found that point of no return. The defendant was incriminating herself more and more! She was becoming more confused. He was pushing her to the end, just like Walter had done on February 27. This murder was beginning to look like premeditation!

"Why didn't you tell Sheriff Gossett that you had made up the story?"

She looked quite confused, as did everyone else in the courtroom, not sure what the question really was. Had he jumped ahead of himself?

"Are you asking me why I made up the story?"

"Yes, that is what I am asking you."

"Because I wanted to avoid being prosecuted! I was scared! I didn't want to go to jail, but I wanted him to stop beating me. I had made more than one call for help in the nine years of marriage. I had left more than once! Not once did anyone answer my calls, especially the weekend of the shooting. Would you have rather I stayed and put up with the beatings? Watch my kids go through it for the rest of my life, which would not have been much longer had he woke up!"

"Mrs. Wagger, I'm asking the questions. You just provide the answers."

Tears filled her eyes again and began to flow down her cheeks. Her face was now drawn and expressed very little hope. The courtroom was filled with sympathetic faces, but how long would that last? Was it for the woman we were all staring at, or just due to the fact that our emotions were all in overdrive?

"Didn't Mr. Wagger show you kindness at times?"

"Yes, sometimes, but not too often!"

"And when you left him, didn't he write you nice letters?"

"Yes, he would write me letters and ask me to come home. He would tell me he loved me and wanted me to continue to be his partner. He wanted us to continue with the marriage!"

Wait a minute! Are we talking about the same man that the prosecution had convinced her, and wanted us to believe, did not love her? Now he was bringing out letters contradicting his own remarks.

"Do you recognize this letter?"

"Yes. Walter wrote me this letter on April 22, 1981."

"Was this the kind of letters he would write to you when you had left?"

"Yes."

"What does this letter say?"

"'Dear Patricia, I'm sorry I made you leave. I want you back home where we can continue to be partners and a family. I'm nothing without you. I know I don't treat you very nice, and I don't know what comes over me. If you will forgive me, I promise to treat you better. Love, Walter.'"

"And didn't he write you another letter of this nature on October 22, 1985?"

"Yes, when I left him and went to Mom's. He brought the letter to me when he came down and got the kids."

"And the third letter — when did you, if you did, get this letter?"

"It came on October 23, 1985. It came in the mail to me at Mom's."

"Would you read this to the court?"

"Yes. 'I'm sorry that I'm not enough for you. That I don't love you enough, and this is the right way to say goodbye. I never did satisfy you in our lovemaking cause you were always thinking of someone else. It was a no damn good love affair anyway."

Just that portion of the letter was enough. She said he then called her and begged her to come home. While many wondered why she stayed, I for one was beginning to understand! He was so insecure, more so about himself than her. His inadequacies, in his mind, were her fault. He accused her of cheating on him. But if she was so bad, why did he drop the divorce proceedings, not once, but twice? Why did he leave his first wife and kids to be with her? Why did he beg her to come home? These were no longer just her words, but Walter's as well, spoken through his handwriting! At the conclusion of this letter, there was a pause that seemed to last an eternity. Mr. Marks paced the floor, rubbing his chin, but before he could ask, she responded.

"Walter always accused me of fooling around on him."

"Mrs. Wagger, didn't you have an affair with Jeremy Brentwood?"

"No, I did not."

"Didn't you try to have an affair with Chad Miller?"

"No, I did not!"

"But you sat in this courtroom and heard him testify that he thought you were trying to entice him into going to bed with you."

"It wouldn't take much to entice someone at the Harald Apartments."

From what we had already heard of those apartments, she was right. It was almost a prerequisite to moving in — getting laid there was as easy as betting against the odds and losing.

"Tell us about the couple from Chicago."

"Someone had put my niece's picture in a magazine, along with my name and address. A lot of people wrote to me, but the letters from the Tates were the only ones I answered."

"Mr. Wagger didn't want you to write to them, did he?"

"At first he said no, but then after he read the letters, he told me to write to them."

"They wrote some pretty explicit things in those letters, didn't they?"

"Yes!"

"Are these the types of letters you wrote back to them?"

"Yes!"

"I'm going to hand you a letter, and I want you to tell me if you received this letter from the Tates."

"No, I did not receive this one."

"Wasn't it written to you?"

"Yes! But the date on it is postmarked after we left Farmtown, and I never got it."

"Mrs. Wagger, I'm going to ask you to read this letter."

She paused. Her voice changed from in control to childlike as she looked to the judge and replied, "Do I have to? This is really bad!"

Judge Kimble asked council to approach the bench. Every eye in the courtroom looked puzzled, everyone straining to overhear what was taking place between them. It was learned that the judge had asked the defense attorneys if they had any objections to their client reading a letter that she claimed she did not receive. After returning to their seats, the defense objected to the defendant reading the letter. She let out a sigh of relief when the judge sustained the objection.

"Mrs. Wagger, is this the type of correspondence you maintained with the Tates?"

"Yes."

"Have you ever seen this letter?"

"No."

"Who was this letter addressed to?"

She looked at the envelope, then the heading of the letter: "Me and Walter!"

"But you don't remember getting this letter either?"

"No!"

"But you did receive letters of this nature from the Tates?"

"Yes!"

The Prosecutor then paused, as if he was looking for another route. God knows he was getting nowhere this way.

"Mrs. Wagger, this letter speaks of oral sex and three or four persons involved in sexual activity, is that right?"

"Yes."

"And these are the kinds of letters written between you and the Tates?"

"Yes."

"The last sentence indicates that a photo was enclosed, is that right?"

"That is what it says, but I don't recall receiving this letter."

"I want you to look at this picture and tell me if you recognize it."

The courtroom was silent, with the exception of a few coughs and the movement of a few people getting restless. No one spoke, nor did anyone leave the courtroom. These were crucial times in the trial.

"No, I don't recognize it."

"You don't recall ever seeing this picture or these people?"

"No!"

"Didn't you engage in unusual sexual activity with the Tates?"

"I'm not saying we didn't."

"Didn't you?"

"Yes!"

"Was that not your idea?"

"No, it was not!"

"Did you take pictures during these unusual sexual activities?"

"Yes, Walter and Adam did!"

"Mrs. Wagger, didn't you keep a photo album of the pictures taken during these unusual sexual activities?"

"No! I didn't! Walter kept it."

"And where is it now?"

"Walter burned part of it, and I burned the rest."

"Weren't those pictures only burned after Walter died?"

"No! They were burned before that happened."

Patricia was not leaning. She was answering the questions short and to the point, giving Mr. Marks no more than he was asking for! Tempers were beginning to flare, giving way only to falling tears. There were times when Mr. Marks came across as hard, disgusted, almost livid, but always determined to ask the same questions over and over again until he had gotten the answer he was seeking, or at least a doctored-up version thereof!

Patricia was used to this. Walter had taken whatever route necessary to hear what he wanted to hear, or maybe he just couldn't take being wrong. This prosecutor must have seemed like a pussycat! Mr. Marks was pacing the floor, rubbing his chin, holding an ink pen, seldom diverting back to his notes to assist in his line of questioning. He had his questions memorized from beginning to end. He seldom looked at the jury, the judge, the defense attorneys, or the spectators. His eyes glared at the defendant as he proceeded.

"Mrs. Wagger, you claim this was all your husband's idea, right?"

"Yes!"

"But didn't your correspondence with the Tates continue even after Walter was dead?"

"They wrote me while I was in jail waiting for this trial."

"How often did you receive letters from them?"

"I don't know, once or twice I guess."

"According to jail records, you received four letters from the Tates in 1987 alone. Is that correct?"

"Yes!"

"Would it be accurate to say you answered those letters the same day you received them?"

"I did answer those letters the same day I received them. I liked them; they were nice people."

"Wasn't writing to the Tates your idea, and didn't Walter just go along with it to please you?"

Well, let's see! Not long before, the Prosecutor had convinced her that Walter did not give a damn about her. Then he brought forth letters Walter had written to her saying otherwise. Now he was implying that her husband had participated in these unusual sexual activities just to please her. Is that why he forced her to have sex with a dog? Just to please her? Did he go to bed with other women and share his wife with other men just to please her? If this were true, Walter Wagger was indeed one hell of a man! Not too bright, but unquestionably a considerate man.

"No!" she quipped loudly. "This was not my idea. Walter never tried to please anyone but hisself."

"Then why did you write to the Tates while you were in jail?"

"I told you! I liked them; they were nice people. I didn't like the things they did, but writing to them was not taking part in their sexual activities."

"Weren't you still corresponding in the same way with the Tates while you were in jail? Weren't the letters the same type as before?"

"They could have been! But they weren't."

She didn't elaborate, nor was she asked to. I couldn't figure out why Mr. Marks had spent so much time on this topic. Whether or not she instigated, was forced, or was a willing participant in unusual sexual activities was not the cause of death. Everyone has a right to his or her own sexual preference. Just because Patricia's was not the ordinary preference, it did not make her a murderer. What made it a bad thing was that, according to her, she was forced to participate. It wasn't the sex, or lack thereof for that matter, that ended the life of Walter Wagger. Or was it? He claimed she was having an affair, so he beat her. She claimed he was beating her, so she did not try to stop her daughter from killing him. It was one vicious cycle! They had rotated with this cycle for nine years. A movement in the courtroom jarred my memory and brought my attention back to the prosecutor.

"Mrs. Wagger, was alcohol a factor in these unusual sexual activities?"

"Yes! We had all been drinking when we did it."

"So you are asking this court to believe that the only reason these activities occurred was because of alcohol?"

"No! I'm not saying alcohol was the only reason they happened. I'm just saying we were drinking when we did them."

"Whose idea was it for you to see a doctor following the shooting?"

"Reverend McMillihen! He thought it was a good idea for me to have my injuries documented."

"Tell us about those injuries."

"I had a scar on my arm where Walter burned me with a cigarette and bruises on my body."

It was a vague answer, but Prosecutor Marks seemed content. That did not mean we would not cross this subject again. He had become notorious for leaving a subject wide open to come back to later.

"You told this court your husband would not let you leave, but hadn't he filed for divorce?"

"Yes, in 1985! He called me on the phone when I was at Mom's. He told me he had filed for divorce, and I told him to go ahead."

"Didn't he indicate the grounds of adultery?"

"Yes! But he also said I had abandoned the kids. I told him to prove it! The kids knew they had been with me, and our kids would tell the truth. He said he had papers giving him custody of the children. I told him that I was going to call and find out for myself. Then he called me back in about five minutes and told me to come home, the beatings would stop, and he still loved me. I believed him, and I came home. He dropped the divorce!"

Prosecutor Marks began to slow down. His questions had gotten away from the shooting, the unusual sexual activities, and how much Walter loved his children and wanted to please his wife. Now he was going back to the letters that Patricia had written to her mother and daughter.

"Mrs. Wagger, when you wrote your mother a letter asking for rat poisoning, didn't you intend to kill your husband then?"

"Yes! Understand that there were many times when I thought about killing Walter, those times when the beatings were so severe and so often! But once they were over, so were my thoughts of killing him. I never wanted Walter dead! I only wanted the beatings to end. I wanted to be married to him, but not the way it was."

"After the shooting, didn't you refuse to talk to the doctors at Minnerstown Medical Center?"

"I was just too upset to talk to them."

"And didn't you refuse to go to Minnerstown and sign those release forms because you knew that, without an operation, Walter would die?"

"No! I didn't have no way there. No one would take me, and the keys to the car were with Walter."

"After you learned that Walter had died, didn't you, on the same day, call his boss and ask him to reissue Walter's check to you?"

"Not the same day. I did want the check reissued, but because we needed the money."

"Didn't you want your husband dead so you could continue to party and have your affairs?"

"That is a lie. I told you over and over: I did not want Walter dead."

"I know, you just wanted the beatings to stop. No further questions."

Well, that was over, and it was time for lunch. However, the defense asked for a chance to redirect, which would not take long. Judge Kimble granted the request.

"Patricia, why didn't you try to stop Megan from shooting Walter?"

"I don't know. We had been through so much that I just wasn't thinking. Me and the kids and Mom – he had abused us all. Not just that weekend, but for all those years. I had called 911 during the weekend, but no one responded. I didn't see any other way out."

"Why did you give a false statement to Deputy Knicely?"

"I was scared, and I guess it all happened so fast that I really didn't know what happened."

"Are you sorry Walter is dead?"

"Yes!"

"Are you responsible for that death?"

"Yes!"

"Was Walter's death premeditated?"

"No! It just happened, and once it did, we couldn't take it back."

"Do you love your children?"

"Yes! And I would never do anything to hurt them."

"Can you see any other way out of the situation with Walter, now that it's over?"

"Now I can, but at the time, there was nothing else to do. I knew in my heart that somebody was going to die. It was just a feeling. I was scared, and I knew if he woke up, he was either going to kill me or the kids. When Megan said she would do it, all I could think of was that it would end the pain. At that moment it was my – our – only way out."

"No further questions."

"I have nothing further, Your Honor," Mr. Marks advised.

"Your Honor, the defense rests."

For Patricia, the line of questioning was now over! Almost four hours on the witness stand, with very little time out. She could no longer defend herself. Anything she had failed to say would never be heard. Anything she had said could not be taken back. The rest was up to the rebuttal witnesses. I watched her closely as she left the witness stand. She had spent the entire day there yesterday. It would seem odd to watch another face after her. There was a certain look about her face – not remorse, not fear, not confidence! I tried to experience her feelings, before the shooting, after the Shooting, now that it was over, but that was impossible! She must have wondered who her real friends were. People she had entrusted with her most intimate thoughts; men to whom she had given herself, if only for moments of passion and kindness; letters she had written to loved ones in private; incidents that occurred in the bedroom and to be kept intimate – were all being held against her! She wasn't so different from the rest of us. Now she stood in a world of her own. How could she feel? Alone!

CHAPTER 27

I watched him closely as he spoke. He did not once allow his eyes to move in the direction of the defendant. I was having a difficult time imagining her with this man. She was attractive in her own way, not beautiful, but, without a doubt, she could have done much better than the first rebuttal witness.

Wade Bradsworth! Finally, there was a face to put with the name. I kept reminding myself that every time this man's name was mentioned, so was the word "alcohol." I knew if she was involved with him, then truly alcohol does make people do things they normally would not do. While the actual picture of Walter Wagger had been nothing more than an imaginary figure to me, the picture my mind was portraying was certainly more than what my eyes were beholding. I was anxious to see just how far this affair had actually gone, according to the gospel of Wade Bradsworth.

He was boisterous as he spoke, not hesitant. He was proud of what he was saying, as though his words were about to become a cure-all. His testimony began.

Assistant Prosecutor Smith set in motion the rebuttal witnesses.

"Mr. Bradsworth, have you ever lived in Appleton?"

"Yes, Sir."

His voice sounded as if his military sergeant was standing in front of him. Mr. Smith looked as if he was affected by the mannerism of this young man.

"In 1987, I moved into the Harald Apartments with Shelby Carder. We lived with her father, Harold Carder."

"Did you ever meet Patricia Wagger?"

"Yes, Sir!"

"Did you strike up an acquaintance with her?"

"I did!"

I had to wonder if Mr. Bradsworth could handle a question that required more than a two-word answer.

"How did that happen?"

"I had been rejected by my girlfriend, so I went to one of the parties at the apartments. The first time I met her was at Mr. Carder's apartment. The people usually gathered there either before or after the party. I had seen her a lot of times, but after that party, we began to strike up an acquaintance."

"Tell us what kind of relationship you and Mrs. Wagger developed."

"Sort of like a boyfriend/girlfriend relationship."

Sort of like! What was that supposed to mean? I guess that was one of those relationships when they really didn't love each other, just liked each other enough to go to bed when there was no one else around, or, in his case, when he had been rejected by his girlfriend! I wanted to ask him the difference between being rejected and being dumped. I really understood what he was trying to say, but what I didn't understand was why he was being apathetic about it all. He was possibly just putting on a front.

"Nothing serious, you know."

"What took place between you and Mrs. Wagger?"

"Well, she would feed me at her home, and then I would go back to the apartments."

"Was there ever a time that you and Mrs. Wagger engaged in sexual activity?"

"We were at a party over at the apartments, and we were both feeling very lonely. I went over to her house, we talked and laughed, and then we went into her bedroom and had sex."

That was about as blunt as one could get. He was too much into his testimony. I already knew he was going to admit to having an affair with Patricia after the prosecution had asked her, "If Wade Bradsworth gets on the stand and says you had an affair with him, he would be telling a lie?"

Those conflicting stories were starting again. It must have been the thing to do: she was to deny, he was to admit! He was the cause of the argument that led up to that fatal day in the Wagger home. Some boyfriend/girlfriend relationship this was. He couldn't even tell her he had wrecked the jeep. Because of him, a marriage, for what it was worth, had ended! Four children had been uprooted, a man was dead, and a mother was facing a charge of murder! But Wade had been rejected!

Truthfully, this boyfriend/girlfriend thing was nothing more than a one-night stand. As I watched his eyes, there was something eerie about this man. He was here strictly for himself, whether it was to brag about what a man he was, to move in on a married woman while the husband was away, or simply in his own defense! He was feeling guilty of wrecking the jeep — another ploy to make Patricia look like the guilty one. Wade Bradsworth, squeaky clean!

Maybe he was here to settle a score! She had ended the boyfriend/girlfriend thing when she found out Walter was coming home. After all, he had already been rejected once! Maybe it was because Walter had Patricia, and Wade would always play second fiddle. Maybe he was feeling guilty! His testimony was not necessarily meant to hurt the defendant, but in no way was it going to help her! Did his story involving the jeep coincide with Patricia's and Megan's?

"I borrowed Mrs. Wagger's jeep to pick up some dishes and things this woman had given me. On the way back home, we were playing around, and the wheels went off the road. The jeep struck a tree."

"What happened when you took the jeep back to Mrs. Wagger?"

"I took the keys back to her, but, being afraid to tell her, I didn't mention it to her. I went back over to the apartment."

Afraid! Afraid of what? In his mind, this was his girlfriend! He was her boyfriend! If he couldn't tell her, then whom could he tell? Or was he really afraid of her husband? Had he possibly heard or seen the tantrums Walter was capable of when somebody dared to cross him?

"After I went back over to the apartment, the kids came over and told me that their mother wanted to see me. So, I went over to her house and talked to her. I told her I was sorry, and if she would call my mother maybe she would take care of it."

If she would call? Now this was a man! He was too afraid to tell a woman he had wrecked her jeep, then he told her to call his mother to take care of it! Fine, upstanding pillar of the community! This was his responsibility! There was still something very mysterious about this man.

He continued: "Before she could call my mom, her husband returned her call. She told him she had wrecked the jeep. She said that her husband was going to kill her if she didn't get it fixed before he came home. She said he wouldn't understand why she let me borrow it."

It all made sense to me; she had reason to be afraid! How, after all the beatings for no reason, was she going to avoid one this time? Patricia informed Walter she had loaned the family jeep to this "acquaintance," and Walter accused her from day one of cheating. Maybe Mr. Wonderful here was revealing to the court that Patricia told Walter she did it to "cover his bacon"

GUSTAVA MARTIN

— this man who did not have the decency to tell her he wrecked the jeep in the first place! If this relationship was boyfriend/girlfriend, why didn't Mr. Bradsworth spare her the beatings and tell Walter himself? Hell, he couldn't even call his own mother to have it fixed! He had a week to take care of it before Walter came home. Instead, he did the manly thing and hid where Patricia could have no contact with him.

Maybe, in a lot of ways, Megan had inherited the "take the blame yourself" motto from her mother. It must have been easier to take a beating for wrecking the jeep rather than admit to letting some man borrow it and bring it back in this condition.

I was hoping the defense would take this witness and dig into him with everything it had. Give this one to cocky little Defense Attorney Roth!

The prosecution had no further questions.

Wade Bradsworth had very shifty eyes that overshadowed his polite guy facade. I only believed about half of what he said, but I had to admit he was pretty damned convincing. No doubt, Patricia had a relationship with this man. It might have even been a one-night stand! But a boyfriend/girlfriend thing? Not unless we were all still in middle school! I insisted on keeping my eyes steadfast on Wade Bradsworth. I wanted desperately to witness remorse from him. Was there any anger toward Walter for having pushed his family this far? Did he harbor any sympathy or guilt for having been the catalyst behind this anguish? Was this man going to show any feelings at all for the person he called "nothing serious" but just like a girlfriend?

I didn't blame him for the entire ordeal. However, I didn't praise him for the role he had played. He was far from innocent, sitting on the witness stand, professing to be the good guy! If Patricia Wagger was guilty of committing adultery, then so was he. If she had lied about wrecking the jeep to save herself, she was protecting him as well. He wasn't man enough to try to fix the damage when it happened, and he sure as hell was not going to fix it now! Patricia had taken the blame, and Walter paid the price!

Wade had used Patricia, and, short of the court paying him to appear here today, he had gotten off scot free! Was there no justice? The two had sat together, drank together, laughed and talked together. In those hours of need, where was he? That final hour of Walter's life, where was he then? As she sat alone in the county jail, where was he then?

Patricia and her family had faced this pain alone! Friendships were torn apart and a family was totally destroyed. The common denominator was Wade having wrecked the jeep!

140

When the defense attorney stood, I had to chuckle that it was none other than Mr. Roth. I wanted to hear him prove this "boyfriend" was as feigned as I perceived him to be.

"Where do you live now?"

"In Florida."

"Do you have a job there?"

"Yes, I do. I'm a commercial shrimperman."

"Now Mr. Bradsworth, you claim that you and Mrs. Wagger were sort of boyfriend/girlfriend, is that right?"

"Yes, I did."

"What do you think caused that to happen?"

"We were two lonely people who needed someone and were just in the same place."

"How many times did you engage in sexual activity with Mrs. Wagger?"

"Just one time!"

I kept looking for some fragment, other than his character, to discredit this man. Come on now! He lied to Patricia on several occasions, including when he told her nothing would happen to the jeep. Then, when he wrecked it, this well-mannered, kind-hearted, lonely man left the scene of the accident and returned the jeep without so much as an "I'm sorry!" I wasn't sure what he was hiding, but I knew there was something!

"How did you get to Upland County for this trial?"

"I arrived on a bus, then a deputy picked me up and brought me here."

"Are you facing any type of criminal charges in Florida?"

"No, Sir! Criminal charges are pending, but I'm not set to go to trial until August."

"What kind of criminal charges are you talking about?"

"Felony charges for the possession of over twenty grams of marijuana."

"Thank you, Mr. Bradsworth. No further questions!"

When the prosecution announced it had no further questions, he was excused. Judge Kimble advised him, just as he had all other witnesses: "You may remain in the courtroom if you desire."

Mr. Bradsworth stepped down from the witness stand, making sure he got the last word in: "Thank you, Your Honor."

During the trial, the courtroom was filled to the maximum capacity, with late comers standing in the hallway. Many were there just to get a glimpse of what was really behind the murder! Once Patricia had testified, the faces seemed to fade. The interest was fading, not so much in the case, but in the testimony!

The shock of her testimony was what most had come to hear. Somehow, I thought they got more than they bargained for.

The negative comments made against Patricia outweighed the positive ones. Somehow, even her socialite neighbors were admitting to seeing nothing. The Harald Apartments were nothing more than a social club with the added luxury of a place to sleep it off. And yes, somebody to sleep it off with! But to those who basically did not belong anywhere else, it was home! I wasn't any better than they were, I just had a different lifestyle. Although, many locals stereotyped the residents there as dirt-bags!

People were free: they could drink when they wanted; sleep with whomever they wanted; fight when they wanted; and in the case of Walter Wagger, abuse their family whenever they wanted, without the fear of being arrested! This lifestyle was an everyday occurrence. It wasn't that people didn't notice, they just didn't want to get involved. It was just a way of life!

This existence was nothing new to Patricia. It had been her way of life since her affair with Walter began. The difference was that here, she wasn't alone! Here, at the Harald Apartments Patricia fit in!

The picture now being painted of her was not necessarily that of an unfit mother or a bad wife, but that of a self-centered woman. She was a woman who was living for herself, and she didn't give a damn who got hurt in the process.

I heard all the reasons she gave for wanting him dead, or at least, for his actions against her and the children to stop – legitimate reasons! But I still struggled with the way she had handled it!

This trial had forced me to feel every emotion I was capable of having. Some I had never used before! Where would these children go if she was convicted? Had they not suffered enough? She had always either taken care of her children or had Megan to take care of them. Her children did not go hungry. They were not mistreated by her. And while she struggled with the oldest son, she claimed to have gone back to that marriage each time she left for fear of losing them. Those kids were all she had to call her own!

There was the thought that she might view this freedom from Walter as a time to live her own life, and the children might suffer from lack of attention from their mother. But Megan would always be there!

Somebody had to suffer the consequences. The beatings would stop, the name-calling would stop, and the sexual abuse would stop! But murder is against all we Americans stand for! Even in the biblical sense, telling us not to kill. But wife- and child-abuse are sickening acts within themselves. It's morally wrong, and it's spiritually wrong! Somehow, that abuse went unnoticed until Patricia and Megan turned on Walter.

Patricia did not exaggerate the abuse. It had not occurred just one time. Walter had not just gotten mad over the jeep, drank too much, and gone ballistic on her! It had been proven. It occurred practically every day of her life with him. She was free from it only while he was away, the fear of it never disappearing!

For nine years, Patricia paid the price for loving Walter. The mistake she made at the age of eighteen would eat away at her until the day she died! Her children were paying for that mistake. Walter met his fate because of that mistake. The only one who knew the real Walter was her father.

Through it all, no matter what my feelings were toward the crime, I knew she was a fighter. She had fought for everything she had, from her children right down to her sanity! This war with Walter was over, but she would always have the battle scars.

CHAPTER 28

The rebuttal witnesses continued following the lunch recess on day nine of the trial.

Walter, at the time of his death, was employed by Darrell Morning, the continuance of the many people who had and would sing the praises of a man they knew only away from his family.

"Mr. Morning, are you employed?"

"Yes, Sir. I own a trucking company out of Virginia."

I had to smile at this gentleman! He appeared to be in his late fifties and had a real southern drawl, and his voice quivered with every word. I had to wonder how many of these people ever once thought that, in a split second, such a change would occur in their everyday lives.

"What type of work does your company do?"

"We lease trucks for Naval Van Lines."

"Did you have the occasion to meet Walter Wagger?"

"Yes, Sir! I was looking for drivers, and I obtained his name from a driving school. I conducted an interview into his past and gave him an examination. He passed it, so I hired him as one of my drivers."

"When did he become employed with your company?"

"On January 3, 1987."

"What sort of pay scale was Mr. Wagger on?"

"He was on salary. After four weeks, they get a commission on everything they do. He worked for two-hundred and fifty dollars a week. Every other check was sent home after the driver received his one hundred dollar withdrawal!"

I was somewhat bewildered at the thought of this man sending money home to support his family. He was being made out to be a saint because he sent home "every other check." According to my quick calculations, his family of five was living on approximately five hundred dollars a month, but subtracting his weekly one hundred dollar withdrawal left him sending home three hundred dollars, providing taxes were not being taken out. With that, his wife was to feed the children and pay the household bills while he, Walter, the good husband, good father, non-violent man, was living on his two hundred dollar withdraw, alone. He was paying no bills, living high on the hog if you asked me! I was not a genius when it came to a budget, but five people surviving on three hundred dollars a month did not add up!

"Mr. Morning, what kind of impression did you have of Walter Wagger?"

"I thought he was a very nice man."

"Were there ever any problems caused on the job by Mr. Wagger?"

That was hardly a fair question, considering the man was on the road most of the time. But the defense did not object!

"No, Sir."

"Did you find him to be violent or quarrelsome in any way?"

"No, Sir! I thought he was a very good employee."

"How did you learn of Mr. Wagger's death?"

"I received a phone call from a lady who didn't tell me who she was. She told me he wouldn't be back to work because he had died."

"Did she tell you anything else?"

"No, Sir. I didn't ask any questions."

"Did you receive another call concerning Walter after his death?"

"Yes, Sir. I received a call from another lady, asking me if I would re-issue his last check to his wife. Our policy states that we do not reissue any checks, and that is what I told the lady."

"Had you talked with Mr. Wagger anytime during the weekend before the shooting?"

"I called him Sunday and told him to stay home for a few days. Business was slow, and I didn't need him to drive for me. He offered to come back to work, but I told him it was not necessary."

Maybe, just maybe, this was the reason for Walter becoming more angered. Patricia said he always became angry when he got laid off or lost his job, even for a short period of time! Somehow, he always blamed his wife. On that weekend, he had told her she was making him miss work. He didn't even tell the truth about that. He supposedly had called his boss asking for time off, asking if his wife knew anyone who could keep his kids! Now, according to Mr.

Morning, he had been the one to place the calls, not Walter. So far, there was no mention of the kids!

I started thinking about the funeral. "This was a family that did not have a pot to urinate in much less the money to bury a body. What was the interaction between the family and friends? How many of these people, who thought he was such a saint, even made an appearance to pay their last respects? Did he have an insurance policy to cover the expenses in the event his wife and stepdaughter would find his death the only way out? It was never mentioned — money didn't seem to be a factor, other than the Wagger family never having any. More questions were left unanswered.

Mr. Morning had been an honest witness, at least as honest as he was capable of being. A job interview that was pertinent for survival — Walter was definitely not going to screw that up. As far as a background check, there was nothing there! Every time anyone had filed any charges against him, including his ex-wife, those charges were always dropped. Most of the time, Walter was just being Walter! That's the way he was. He never robbed a bank or shot anyone, he wasn't a stalker, and he was never picked up for driving under the influence. The only crimes Walter had ever committed were drinking too much and trying to maintain control of his household, no matter what the cost! Most of those accusations went unreported, some were dropped before they hit the courts, and others were unfounded. It was his way of life!

Defense Attorney Roth approached the witness in an effort to pinpoint the actual number of times Mr. Morning had encountered Walter Wagger.

"I saw him around ten times, from his interview to the last day he worked for me."

"Had you ever talked with him after the interview?"

"Not really, I only spoke to him now and then."

"During the time he worked for you, how often was he on the road?"

"Sometimes for two weeks at a time."

"Did you ever see the results of the investigation conducted into the background of Walter Wagger?"

"No, I did not."

"Did Walter Wagger ever pistol whip you?"

"No, Sir!"

"Did he ever spit in your face?"

"Never!"

"Did he ever complain to you about his wife and kids?"

"No."

Mr. Roth was attempting to establish how difficult it would be for Mr. Morning to see the violence in a man to whom he was barely close enough to speak. How could he hear Walter complain about anything from a distance? Walter was definitely the epitome of a con artist! But then again, with this new job, maybe he was trying to change. Maybe he saw this as his break — his chance to make a better life for his family. Maybe the money he was keeping for himself, twice the amount he was sending home to his family, was being saved! He knew that way it would not be spent foolishly, like on one of his wife's many men, or to feed his children. If that was the case, his newfound chance lasted only seven weeks before it cost him his life!

As Mr. Morning stepped down from the witness stand, a ten-minute recess was granted. For most of those who had been in the courtroom for the past few days, the thought of the worst being over was foremost in our minds. One could not determine where the prime rebuttal witness was going to come in, but was certain there was one hanging in the ballast. When was the praising of Walter Wagger by someone other than his family going to stop? Many who had sworn before the court spoke of a kind man, a nice man, a good father and husband, a good employee. That man was now gone! There was no cause for fear of him, so where was the sympathy for the family who had endured his kindness all these years?

I still harbored compassion for Walter, a man I never knew and would not have heard of had it not been for his murder. Had he died a natural death, in an accident, or by suicide, he would still be non-existent! He had lived a life controlled by a demon that forced him to use violence to control what was his. He could not control his own life, but he breathed to control others. He had caused so much physical, emotional, and mental pain to people as innocent as his children! But in his mind, he was not going to let them go wild. He enjoyed drinking, and if he wanted to, he could stop anytime. On that fatal night, he enjoyed drinking too much. The alcohol he loved so much left him in a condition where he never knew what hit him — the bullet that ended his life!

For Walter, the pain was over. The demon was gone. For those he left behind, it was just beginning. Many of those praising him now had their own negative encounters with Walter, but now that he was dead, they were paying tribute to him. In the finest fashion, maybe it was guilt. Maybe it was sympathy for a life taken so young and without warning. But I was leaning more toward revenge on Patricia for these witnesses' past experiences with her.

A year ago, this family was unknown, except for the many calls to the 911 center. But, thanks to the murder, the media coverage had made "Wagger" a

147

household name.

A coworker of Walter's was next to take the stand; Mr. Smith began.

"Please state your name and where you are employed."

"Timothy Hardwood, and I am a truck driver for Naval Van Lines."

"Did you know Walter Wagger?"

"Yes, we drove truck together. I mean we were driving partners."

"How long did you drive together?"

"About two weeks."

"Did you ever see Walter consume alcohol while you were driving together?"

"No. Anytime we ever went out, he mostly drank Coke."

Now we are going to dispute the fact he drank. Maybe it was a part of his change! I was convinced Walter wore more than one face, two of which were the one worn around his acquaintances, which appeared kind, hardworking, an all around good guy, and the one his friends saw, which only showed anything bad when he was drinking. He was good in front of those he worked with and for and kind to his friends, going as far as sharing his wife with some of them and taking theirs in return. With his family, he had to prove nothing, no one to impress. He had only to maintain control! This third face that his family saw was loud and abusive, but also sometimes gentle and kind! The first two must have kept the last one bottled up! When that face appeared, his wife and children could not go far enough to get away from it. It was unleashed with a vengeance! What a miserable life! It was difficult enough to be one person, let alone three.

"Did Mr. Wagger ever talk to you about family problems?"

"The last day we were on the road together, he asked me if he could borrow three hundred dollars. He said his wife let someone borrow the jeep, and the guy had wrecked it. He needed the money to get the jeep fixed."

Discrepancies again! Mr. Bradsworth said Patricia told Walter she had wrecked the jeep. And if Patricia had not told him how bad the jeep was, how did Walter know the dollar amount to borrow to have it fixed?

"Did you give him the money?"

"Yes, Sir, the day he came home."

"Do you believe Walter Wagger was a violent and quarrelsome man?"

"I never saw him that way."

With no further questions from the prosecution, Assistant Defense Attorney Roth stepped up to the stand. Both he and Mr. Ray were beginning to look a little tired and weary. I personally was not pleased with the job they had done in defending Patricia. But I knew it was difficult for anyone to defend the taking of a life. The life of a twenty-nine-year-old mother of four lay in their hands! There was little left for them to do at this point, except make these witnesses less credible than those they had presented. They needed to leave enough doubt in the jury's mind as to what verdict to bring back.

What should have been their greatest victory passed them by when Prosecutor Marks turned around the horrible, sickening, devastating, and mortifying life of which Patricia had testified. He had made her life more of a choice than a force! I knew when the defense did not fight back, its battle was over.

The jury would have to decide, if they had not already done so, which side was most convincing, who they believed. Was she an adulterous, partying woman who left her children for self-gratification? Was he a kind man who never meant harm to anyone? Was he really the monster Patricia, her mother, and Megan had made him out to be? Was she an abused woman with no self-esteem who was pushed into committing this crime by a love affair gone bad? The defense was continuing to try, but was it too late in the game?

"How long had you known Walter Wagger?"

"Two weeks."

"Did you ever see him with his wife or children?"

"No, Sir."

"The actual time you spent with him was on the road, is that correct?"

"Yes, Sir, just those two weeks."

Same questions, different witness – that was the pattern we were now following!

149

CHAPTER 29

Defense Attorney Roth was aggressive and shrewd. He always managed to come back with something, if for no other reason than to break the monotony!

While he might not have always discredited the witness, he always left us questioning the truth in what they were saying. Of course, there were only two testimonies that mattered anyway—that of Megan, who was totally honest, and that of Patricia, who did not fabricate the abuse! Many times, the same questions were asked, but the answers weren't always exact. Their descriptions of the period of time leading up to the shooting, the conversation between Megan and Patricia prior to the shooting, and the shooting itself swayed somewhat. But these two witnesses, key witnesses, never swayed on the abuse!

The only real question was whether Patricia had forced Megan to pull the trigger. I knew how people viewed Walter and Patricia, but how had Megan been viewed? To me, it was not a forced issue! No doubt, Patricia had asked Megan to shoot Walter, but had she forced her to do it? Perhaps it was a sympathy killing—Megan's sympathy for her mother, or the fear of someone other than Walter dying when he woke up!

It had been more than a year since the shooting had occurred, but dear God, how could so many forget the facts?

The prosecution's witnesses had outweighed the defense's by three to one. Who was the real victim here?

Court was adjourned until 9:00, Wednesday morning.

CHAPTER 30

I was in a deep sleep when the clock downtown struck midnight. That had never fazed me until I listened to testimony concerning the time frame on February 27, 1987. It was during that midnight hour when the plan was put into play — the last-minute decision to end the physical, mental, verbal, and sexual abuse of Patricia Wagger, to end the physical and verbal abuse to other members in that household, and to end the life of twenty-nine-year-old Walter Wagger!

Time seemed to be lost between 11:30 that night, when Walter came home and passed out in the chair, and 12:45 the following morning, when Deputy Maracos arrived on scene. Time meant everything now! Time was all she had!

As long as this trial would take, and during the time it would take the jury to reach a verdict, Patricia remained innocent by law. The waiting period must have been overpowering. For nine years, Walter controlled her life. Now two defense attorneys and two prosecuting attorneys would place that control into the hearts and hands of a twelve-member jury.

Day after day, hour after hour, minute by minute. Sitting in jail, anticipating the outcome!

Only she could know the full nine years of her life with Walter. Others had listened to the allegations and envisioned a small portion of it. Unfortunately, for her, she had always been present.

Why was it that those who knew so little told so much? Those who had seen him at his finest told so little. Those talking the most were leaving an amazing impact that did not simulate the man Patricia and Megan described. For days, I had watched sitting in the front of the courtroom nestled between her attorneys. She showed little, if any, emotion, except when she testified, when

151

she brought forth and relived the entire nine years in front of many. She only spoke when spoken to. Sometimes she was mesmerized, somewhat frustrated, at the accusations the prosecution was making. Her husband never loved her, he only wanted the children! But instead of coming off the stand at the prosecutor, she responded when advised to do so. I had to question how so many people could be so right about Walter. If all of what they said about him was true, that in turn, would mean that Patricia and Megan were wrong. Who really knew him best?

Then there was Megan. In retrospect, I pondered her testimony and the admittance of "only minor injuries" — even so, injuries that should have never happened! She knew somebody was going to die. She was helpless! By the time the shooting occurred, she had taken care of three children, her grandmother, and her mother. For as much as she hated Walter for the way he treated them, she still took the time to fix him food before he passed out. Did she do it for him or to help her mother? Did it really matter? She had spoken of killing Walter to her friend in school after he had beaten her. She did want that character he portrayed dead!

Megan was only a year old when Walter entered her life. She was exempt from a large portion of the abuse, but only because Walter refused to let her live with him and her mother. She had visitation with her mother, but only when Patricia came to visit, or when Patricia left Walter and came home. Then at last, Walter agreed to let Megan and her grandmother come to live with them. Megan became a part of her mother's life that did not involve short visits or correspondence by mail. Now, when her mother spoke, she heard her. When her mother cried, she saw it. When her mother suffered abuse from Walter, Megan felt the pain. Yes, at last she was a part of her mother's life, but what a price she had paid!

What were the alternatives? Megan could not pack up and leave. She loved her brothers and sister. She loved her grandmother. She loved her mother. She suffered right along with them. Her stepfather loathed her very being.

She told of those events leading up to the Walter's death — the repetitious beatings, name-calling, and drinking. She was eleven years old! In her mind, her mother was dating Wade Bradsworth. Wade thought she was too.

Megan had watched as her stepfather hit her mother and called her a bitch, among other names. She watched as he hit her grandmother. She felt the anger when she and Colin did not go to school after two nights of ongoing fighting.

Walter had told Patricia to be gone, but when he left, he took her exit with him — both sets of car keys in his pocket!

The prosecution stated this was not a remote area; she could have gotten help. Of course, we saw how many were coming to her rescue now, so what made anyone think they would have helped her then?

How frightening it must have been to know in your heart somebody was going to die! Loneliness beyond human understanding. Helplessness with no end in sight. Living for the moment, knowing damn well this was the last time someone was going to know the wrath of Walter.

Megan knew it, too, as she cooked a meal at 11:00 that night, knowing it was going to be somebody's last! Walter never woke up to have that meal!

Megan had lay in bed, knowing her mother was sitting on a loaded gun — a gun she planned on using on somebody. She knew somebody was not going to wake up when the morning sun came over the horizon.

To an eleven-year-old child, it must have been a process of elimination. She hated Walter for everything! Not just against her, but mostly the way he treated her mother, her brother, and her grandmother. Who was going to die depended on Megan. Could she do it?

The weekend had come and gone without a kind word being spoken. There was nowhere to run this time. Thanks to the alcohol, the midnight hour brought a peaceful sound — a sound that had not echoed through those walls since Walter arrived home. His welcome home, after a two-week absence, was an instantaneous burst of loud voices, accusations, beatings, and name-calling, which led to drinking! Walter had made several attempts to find one thread of evidence from the residents at the apartments that Patricia was having an affair with Wade. He had humiliated her in front of those who claimed to be her friends. At last, it all ended when Megan once again eased her mother's mind. I could still hear her voice when she said, "I knew somebody was going to die and I didn't want it to be Mom."

She had taken the responsibility most adults would never know. Megan was street-wise beyond her years!

Someday, given the opportunity, Megan would be the perfect mother. I imagine she will be very choosy when it comes to selecting someone to call her husband, someone to father her children. Someday, the abuse and this ordeal will be behind her. What was defined as a family to her in the early years will reign with the highest of emotions for the rest of her life. Someday, someone will see and accept Megan for what she truly is: a wise, wonderful person who had endured more in one year than any child should be subjected to in a lifetime.

For Megan, the lesson was a difficult one. I hope that, no matter where she goes, she will always remember that she acted upon the request of her mother.

These two shared a dream – someday, the abuse would end, and they could be together without consequences. Whether or not the choice was totally hers, she made that dream come true.

I imagined her lying in bed, trying to put the scenes of those last three days behind her, being awakened by a mother too scared to finish what she had started, knowing in her mind somebody was going to die. Just as she lay in bed awaiting the outcome of the shooting, on this night, Megan was lying in bed awaiting her mother's future.

CHAPTER 31

The rebuttal witnesses continued on day ten.

We were taken back to the previous life of Walter Wagger, before he moved his family to the Harald Apartments, before "welfare" became such a household word.

Greg Wallace recalled his first encounter with Walter.

"I was shop foreman for Mooreover Drilling. Walter came into the shop in September 1984, looking for a job. He accepted the job on the condition that he would work everyday. He was employed until his layoff in January 1986.

"In all the time Walter worked for you, did you ever observe him intoxicated?"

"No, Sir."

"What type of employee was he?"

"He was a good employee. He worked hard and missed very few days of work during his stay."

"Do you believe that Walter was a violent and quarrelsome man?"

"No, Sir."

Defense Attorney Roth asked only one question of this witness: "You don't believe Walter was a quarrelsome man on the job, is that correct?"

"Yes, Sir. That's the only place I ever saw him."

Walter was indeed termed a good and hardworking man while he was on the job. Maybe he was! When he tried, he had no problems finding employment. But what prompted him to change so much when he came in contact with his family? Was his wife the one thing that brought about that change? She wasn't the only one who suffered when his demon came to life. The anger and abuse went from his children to his mother-in-law, from the furniture to the animals! At work, Walter must have been a gift from God, but at home, he was a monster from Hell!

How and where it all started, nobody seemed to know for sure! So far, nobody spoke of the environment in which Walter had grown up. Little had been said about the first trip on the love roller coaster between he and Patricia. The impression was given that his life started when, while married, he began his love affair with Patricia, the second time. Nobody knew where it began, but by now, everyone interested knew where it ended!

The next witness also had worked with Walter at Mooreover Drilling. His testimony would prove to be no different from those that preceded it.

Oran Briggs testified that Walter showed up for work everyday unless he had requested the time off.

"Did you ever see Walter intoxicated or consuming alcohol?"

"No, I did not."

"Did you ever have any problems with Walter?"

"The only problem I ever had with him wasn't really with him but with his wife and kids. She often brought him to work, and the kids would run through the shop while she followed after her husband. There came a time when we finally had to stop it."

"Did he ever borrow any money from you?"

"Yes, on several occasions, but he always paid it back."

Walter Wagger — an interesting specimen to say the least. Even his ex-wife gave a good impression of him. The picture painted by his coworkers and employers was much more tranquil than the one painted by his wife and kids. All the way down the line, Patricia and the children had been to blame for his failures and problems. Somewhere, at sometime, there must have been some good in him. Apparently, that was on the job. When he felt the anger demon surfacing, he just went home. Home! A place where beatings, name-calling, vulgar language, and drinking were expected! Walter was the boss there. He was in control, the leader and the maker. What he said, what he did, whom he did it to — it was all permissible, soon forgiven because Walter made the rules! Home was a place where he could not be fired or laid off. No matter what he did, home was always the place he could come back to. The only thing that stood between Walter and home was death.

In 1978, Walter left his marriage to Charlene and their two kids to begin his new life with Patricia. What a life it must have been. When the relationship between he and Patricia began, he saw another chance. Maybe a renewed hope. Certainly a new world. A woman who had been lodged in his mind since their very first encounter years before. A life where love was proclaimed, but not often felt. When Patricia spoke of "making love" with Walter, it either was in anger or included other people, the dog, or the extension. Anyway she described it, it sounded like abuse! Many had gotten on the witness stand to sing their praises of Walter, the man they knew as one who showed up for work everyday, worked hard while on the job, always paid back borrowed money, was never violent or quarrelsome, and never consumed alcohol. These people did not know him as a father, a husband, or even a lover. So what caused the drinking? Surely, after all those years of partaking of what he enjoyed, he must have known what actions he possessed! Who or what prompted him to become violent and quarrelsome? Who was this man?

Walter lived in a world where he never gave, and peace did not exist! I wondered if he was at peace now. The pain and torture of Walter was over. The hurt, the abuse, and the memory thereof would be a burden to all he left behind!

CHAPTER 32

Morning eleven started out as Prosecutor Marks introduced us to their chosen psychologist, who would enlighten the court with his opinion of whether or not Patricia Wagger suffered from Battered Woman Syndrome.

Cecil Androtti, a professor of psychology at Minnerstown University, specialized in forensic pathology.

"Dr. Androtti, have you ever conducted evaluations on women who suffer from the Battered Woman Syndrome?"

"Yes. Several during the last ten years."

"Have you studied the Battered Woman Syndrome, and if so, can you give us some of the symptoms?"

"Yes. I have read several books on the subject and have done quite a bit of research. The women have low self-esteem and are victims of episodic abuse. Jealousy plays a major part with the man. Causes, other than jealousy, include alcohol and isolation, meaning they are moved around a lot and kept from their families."

For someone who had been called by the prosecution, he was certainly playing a prominent role for the defense. He was describing the life Patricia had testified to during her nine years with Walter. If Mr. Marks was trying to insinuate that Patricia did not fit this profile, I wished him good luck.

Dr. Androtti continued: "They can never go anywhere because the man will take the keys to the vehicles. They live in fear of losing their children and being beaten and alone."

Well, if the story we had already heard was not true, the Wagger children, Mrs. Billingston, and Patricia had either read a lot about this topic or had very vivid imaginations. Theirs was a story that held true, according to the experts!

"Did you ever conduct an evaluation on the defendant, Patricia Wagger?"

"Yes. I did so after the shooting."

"And what did that evaluation consist of?"

"I reviewed her records, conducted two interviews with her, then conducted my evaluation."

"Where, and for how long, did this evaluation last?"

"We met at my office in Minnerstown; it lasted for about five hours."

"Would you explain the type of evaluation you conducted on Mrs. Wagger?"

"First, I gave her a test to view her personality that consisted of five hundred and fifty true/false questions. This is the most widely recognized test, and each response is based on statistics. The test revealed that she acts out her personality, then thinks about the situation later. It showed that she is an insensitive person and impulsive, acting only for the moment. At that point, the test also ruled out depression and post traumatic stress."

I wanted to know when this test had been conducted. It must have been some test. Not that I doubted its validity, but proving that Patricia was not only instrumental in the death of her husband, but was also not depressed about it, through a series of true/false questions hardly seemed rational.

Dr. Androtti further stated that other tests he conducted proved that Patricia did suffer from the Battered Woman Syndrome — there was no doubt in his mind. This simply meant that, for the first time in this trial, the prosecution and defense had actually agreed on something.

"Dr. Androtti, do you believe this murder was premeditated or committed in self-defense?"

"I believe she had thought about it. She had made the statement that if he tried to take the kids or if she got the chance, she would shoot him. As far as self-defense, that is difficult to answer. Self-defense means in imminent danger. What choices do they have, and what strength do they have? Women who suffer from the Battered Woman Syndrome often look at this differently. After a long period of abuse, they kill at that point, not for the death, but for the pain to stop."

From his research, Dr. Androtti had concluded these women put up with the abuse for so long that, when the chance presents itself, the strength and courage are there. They do not think about what will happen down the road. They act for the moment! In that case, Patricia was no different from any other woman who had been abused. She had found the chance, so the strength and courage to do something about it followed!

"So, do you, or do you not, believe this was self-defense or premeditated?'

"Mrs. Wagger admitted to talking about killing her husband for over two years. She said she was just sorry she had not done it herself. She had characteristics of a battered woman, but those homicidal characteristics were not there on February 27."

Defense Attorney Roth immediately objected on the grounds that Dr. Androtti was not there at the time of the shooting. He could not professionally give his opinion as to whether or not she had acted in self-defense. The objection was sustained, and the prosecution had no further questions.

Mr. Roth had that look of "let me at him." He was ready for this one! At least I hoped so. As each witness stepped down from the stand, the defense was running out of time. Even though objections were being sustained and comments were being stricken from the record, the damage had been done. How could anyone expect the jury to forget those comments already made?

"Dr. Androtti, did Patricia indicate low self-esteem, which is typical of a battered woman?"

"I don't recall anytime she possessed low self-esteem."

"Now, these tests were given to Patricia after she was no longer in a battered situation, is that correct."

"Yes."

"In fact, she was employed at the time she took the test, is that correct?"

"Yes. She did admit to me that she felt better about herself."

"When exactly did you conduct these tests?"

"This month: June 1988."

"Wouldn't the self-esteem be higher once they were no longer in that situation?"

"Most definitely!"

Defense Attorney Roth had earned some points this time. After all, how was she supposed to react a year after the shooting? A year after the pain had stopped? I realized this was not some sort of score keeping sport, but at times, it seemed like one. Especially now, this close to the end. It wasn't about who played the best. In this case, the only thing that counted was who won. This was not about how well you played the game. It was all about who crossed the finished line first.

The next witness would prove to break the monotony and find a space for some humor – unintentionally, of course!

Gertrude Solene brought the term "country bumpkin" to life. The prosecution asked her numerous times to speak up, and that was just in giving

160

her name. It took sometime in getting an answer to the first question. She possessed a look of disgust at the slightest notion of even being here. Maybe she thought that if she spoke softly enough, the prosecutor would become frustrated and ask no more questions. WRONG!

"How do you know Patricia Wagger?"

"She and me are cousins."

"Were you acquainted with Walter Wagger?'

"If you mean did I know him, yes!"

"Did you do much socializing with the Waggers?"

"I'm not sure what you mean."

"Were you ever at their house, or were they ever at yours?"

"Yes, we went to visit quite a bit!"

"Did you ever see Patricia with bruises or a black eye?"

"Yes, many times. But I don't know how she got them."

"Did the two of you ever talk about Walter beating her?"

"After she went to jail, she told me that Walter had put the stripes on her back."

Stripes? Where did that come from? During Patricia's testimony, she never spoke of stripes. I knew, in due time, I would find out just what Gertrude Solene was speaking of, but I was in no mood for guessing games.

"Did you ever ask her where she got the black eye?"

"No!"

"Mrs. Solene, did you ever see any pictures with Mrs. Wagger?"

"We looked at pictures a lot, but I guess the one's you are talking about are the ones with people partially dressed! Some naked!"

"Were any of these people familiar to you?"

"I knew Patricia and Walter, that's all."

"Mrs. Solene, do you know who those pictures belonged to?"

"She never said. They were in her photo album, so I guessed they were hers."

"Other than them being partially dressed or naked, was there anything else unusual you saw?"

"Well, there was people doing oral sex."

"Did you ever ask her who these people were, or did she ever tell you?"

"She said it was just some people she wrote to. They sent her pictures, and she would send them pictures."

Of what? It didn't seem to me that there was much in her life to boast about. What kind of pictures did she send? Walter mad? Walter being abusive?

Walter drunk? Walter passed out? Not pretty pictures!

"Were there other pictures in the album, other than the ones you've already told us about?"

"Well, there was a picture of a dog."

"Did you ever talk with Mrs. Wagger about the dog?"

"Not at first, but later she told me that Walter had brought home the dog and made her go into the bedroom. She played around with the dog, and then she had sex with the dog."

"Where was Walter while the two of you were looking at these pictures?"

"Outside with my husband."

""What happened after you and Mrs. Wagger looked at those pictures?"

"You mean what did we do?"

"Yes."

It was quite humorous to hear someone other than the attorneys asking the questions.

"We just sat around and talked."

"Did the four of you spend anytime together?"

"You mean me and Patricia and Walter and my husband?"

"Yes!"

"Yes," she answered.

"Did you consume any beverage containing alcohol?"

"I guess you mean was we drinking?"

"Yes, that's what I mean."

"Yes, we was drinking."

"Was there any type of sexual activity that night?"

"Yes, we had sex."

"Can you tell us how that happened?"

She looked puzzled as the courtroom filled with laughter. Without so much as a smile, she replied, "Don't you know?"

"I mean who had sex?" Mr. Marks was finally figuring out that if he was going to get home in the next few days, he was going to have to come down to her level.

"Patricia went to bed with my husband, and I went to bed with Walter."

"Whose idea was it to go to bed that way?"

"I'm not sure. Patricia asked me about switching, and hell, by that time we were all too drunk to care."

The spectators began to laugh. Judge Kimble buried his head far beyond his arm. Up to that point, through all the laughter in the courtroom, he had maintained that sober mood. He had such a pleasant face, and for the first time I saw those pearly white teeth. Prosecutor Marks paced the floor and waited patiently for silence to intervene.

"Whose idea was it to switch?"

"I don't know. Patricia asked me first."

"Did you see Mrs. Wagger and your husband in bed together?"

"No, but I could hear them."

"Where were they?"

"Patricia and my husband were in the bedroom at our house. Me and Walter were on a mattress in the living room floor."

"How would you describe Walter's actions while the two of you were in the living room, and his wife, along with your husband, was in the bedroom?"

"First of all, he was a little nervous."

"What kind of response did he give?"

"You mean did he act like he wanted to have sex?"

Once again, the courtroom was roaring with laughter until Prosecutor Marks interrupted.

"Your Honor, this is not a comedy routine. I cannot continue to question this witness if those in the courtroom do not keep silent."

Judge Kimble removed his hand from in front of his face. After pulling himself together, he stated, "These outbursts will not be tolerated. If they persist, I will clear the courtroom."

"Mrs. Solene, did it take any encouraging by you to make Mr. Wagger engage in sexual activity?"

"At first he wasn't anxious, but then he came around and everything was fine."

"Was this the first time you and your husband engaged in this type of sexual activity with the Waggers?"

"Yes, but it wasn't the last! The next time, we went to their house at Cove Corner. Patricia called me a couple of times, then Walter called my husband several times after that, so we finally went down! We all sat and looked at the photo album together, and I saw more pictures. We started drinking and all had sex on the bed together. I had sex with Walter, and my husband had sex with Patricia."

"Whose idea was it this time?"

"Nobody's really. We just all went into the bedroom together. Nobody forced nobody either time."

"Did you ever talk with Mrs. Wagger about the dog?"

"She once showed me the scratch marks on her back. She wasn't really upset, but that was a good while after she had sex with the dog."

"Did the sexual activity between the four of you ever happen again?"

"No. I guess we had enough! But then again, right after that, they moved away."

"Did you ever see Walter violent or abusive?"

"Yes! One time he had been drinking and got mad. He started calling Patricia names. Then he went outside, and I followed him to give him a wet washcloth. He started calling me bad names, but then, when he saw it was me, he said he was sorry, he thought it was Patricia."

"Mrs. Solene, did you ever meet the Tates?"

"Yes. Only once at Cove Corner."

"Did you know how they met the Waggers?"

"Well, Patricia told me they got her name from a magazine and wrote to her. They wanted her and Walter to come and visit them, but she said Walter wouldn't go, so she invited them to come and visit."

"Did you and Mrs. Wagger ever talk about the photo album after you saw it the last time at her house?"

"I went to see her after she went to jail, and I asked her about it. She said it was in her dresser drawer in the house at Appleton. Then recently, I asked her about it, and she said her boyfriend had burned it."

Once again, we were at a standstill. I kept waiting for the prosecution to pull out that photo album and other mementos from this relationship. I was more interested in the husband/wife relationship than I was the extramarital affairs. I understood how difficult and embarrassing this was for everyone. When people like Gertrude spoke on the witness stand, they were airing not only Patricia and Walter's dirty laundry, but their own as well. Sex was a topic that very seldom left the house in this town, much less was discussed so candidly in front of so many strangers. The Waggers had one thing in common: their desire to experiment when it came to sex!

Prosecutor Marks paused for a moment then had no further questions.

"Mr. Ray, Mr. Roth, your witness."

"Thank you!" Mr. Roth spoke as he stood to face the witness.

"Now Mrs. Solene, may I call you Gertrude?"

"I guess so! Everyone else does."

"Okay Gertrude, had you seen Mrs. Wagger more than once with a black eye?"

"Yes, several times!"

"Did you ever see Walter mistreat his wife?"

"Well, he quarreled with her a lot and called her a lot of bad names that I wouldn't call nobody."

"You stated that it was Patricia's idea to switch partners, but do you know what Patricia and Walter talked about before they arrived at your house, or before you arrived at theirs?"

"No."

"Did your husband ever tell you what he and Walter talked about while they were outside?"

"No."

"Did you rape Walter either of the times that the two of you went to bed together?"

"I hope not! He was a lot bigger than me."

"You stated that Walter wasn't anxious at first. Why do you think that was?"

"I think he was afraid that my husband was going to come out of the bedroom and beat the hell out of him."

"Did he show any reluctance at all to participating in the sexual activity with you?"

"No!"

"Have you any idea what kind of conversation took place between Patricia and Walter concerning the Tates?"

"No."

"Nothing further."

Gertrude looked relieved until Prosecutor Marks stood back up and asked for a few more questions.

"Did Patricia show any anger when she spoke with you about the dog?"

"No."

"Did she ever tell you her husband beat her?"

"No, we went to the bathroom and stuff together, to where she could have told me without Walter hearing, but she never said nothing about it."

"Did you ever see Walter beat his wife?"

"No. But I know he could get pretty violent when he was drinking."

Gertrude was very polite as she breathed her sigh of relief in stepping down from the witness stand. At last, this part was over. How much damage had she done? I guess it depended on what the prosecution was trying to prove. Her testimony was living proof that Patricia and Walter engaged in extramarital activities together, but then again, it was no surprise. Walter had shared

Patricia with at least one friend and one coworker. Other men had sworn Patricia had gone to bed with them, but Gertrude admitted to sleeping with and having sex with Walter. Gertrude was the only proof that Patricia had willingly engaged in sex with any other man than Walter.

Walter had been exempt from all the embarrassment his wife was now going through while she, the one left behind, was working like hell to defend her actions, still tangled in the web created by him — or at least shared with him!

We were at a stage where every witness seemed to be related either to Walter or to Patricia. What a small world!

Juanita Wagger, wife of Walter's brother and sister to Walter's ex-wife Charlene — see what I mean? — was next to testify. The first question asked was whether she had kept in touch with Walter and Patricia.

"Yes. We saw them generally twice a month."

"Did you ever see Walter abuse his wife?"

"No!"

"Was there ever a time when Walter was passed out that you, or anyone near you, tried to wake him up?"

"Yes, once he had been drinking a lot, and I tried to wake him, but it was almost impossible."

"Did Mrs. Wagger ever talk to you about being beaten by her husband?"

"No."

Before the defense had a chance to question Juanita, Judge Kimble called for an adjournment until 9:00 the following morning.

I sat alone in my apartment, trying to remember all that had been said during the course of the day. I knew the end was near!

So many had spoken of never having seen Walter intoxicated. Most of them were people he worked with. However, during testimony with family members and friends, the word "drunk" came up quite frequently.

It wasn't so much what had occurred between Patricia and Walter in their past, but more importantly what happened that weekend, beginning Saturday and ending early Tuesday morning. Although, I would be the first to admit, it was their past that led up to that night.

As for Patricia, she never claimed to be the perfect wife. She also never admitted to having given Walter reason for the abuse.

I had no doubt that from day one, the abuse was prevalent in their household. Every time I closed my eyes, I saw Megan's face. It made me angry when I thought about Patricia, Megan, Colin, Mrs. Billingston, and the abuse.

When I saw Megan, I saw deprivation — not so much of material things, but of truly knowing the love of a father. Walter had the chance to provide that love to Megan, but he couldn't even be a decent father to his own children. Megan was so busy taking care of everyone else, she never had time for a life of her own.

Patricia had shed tears of ridicule when she spoke of her life in that torture chamber.

While Patricia, Megan, and Mrs. Billingston all revealed the abuse they had either witnessed or received, the description of Walter from those who spoke highly of him far outweighed the beast the three of them had portrayed.

Walter had molested those people who cleaned his home, cooked his meals, made his bed, and slept with him.

But one day, without warning, he was gone. When Patricia finally realized he was no longer going to be there, she cried and remarked she did not know what she would do without him. Through it all, she called it love!

CHAPTER 33

Once again, I woke to a perfect summer day — birds singing, sun shining, and temperatures well above normal. We had not experienced one day of rain since the trial began more than a week ago.

For a moment I had forgotten. Forgotten what was facing me! Forgotten what was facing a woman my age who, in reality, had lived twice as much as I had. It probably seemed like twice as long, what she had gone through in her twenty-nine years, especially that last night. I prayed to God it was an experience that I would never know! What was facing Megan and the other three children?

It was not getting any easier with time, just as the life of the Wagger family did not get easier as time went on.

No matter whose story we listened to, the truth remained the same – there was a family shattered by abuse, a man shattered by a demon, and a woman shattered by love!

Who was right or who was wrong was not a decision this court would ever be able to make. None of us had ever even imagined such moments of outrage, much less struggled to live through them. None of us heard the verbal abuse. None of us felt the physical abuse. But then again, none of us knew what went on when Walter was away. Even being of sound mind, none of us could possibly understand what had transpired during this marriage. Yet, twelve of the people sitting in the courtroom would soon have to choose sides. Twelve handpicked to take the words of both sides, often conflicting testimony, and decide if Patricia Wagger was responsible for the murder of her husband, Walter. That would mean finding, without a doubt, that she forced her daughter to pull the trigger. Did being responsible warrant first degree murder? Would the decision have been less complicated had she just shot him herself?

Another day, another witness!

I, along with everyone else in the courtroom, faced the judge, attorneys, the defendant, and the jury.

Defense Attorney Ray had no questions for the witness who had left the stand at the close of court the day before. He stated to the judge that the prosecution could call their first witness of the day.

This trial had begun to take its toll on everyone, even Mr. Marks, who wasted no time getting started.

The first witness of the day was one for whom we had all been waiting. A tall, young, blonde man approached the witness stand. Now, at the age of twenty-one, he was the only affair Patricia admitted to having. The relationship had lasted only a short time before Walter's promise to change took her away.

"Your Honor, the State calls David Vincent. Are you acquainted with the defendant, Patricia Wagger?"

"Yes, Sir. I am."

"Did you have an occasion to go to Wheeler County with her?"

"Yes, Sir. I did."

I had to smile as he testified. He spoke as if he was proud to have been associated with Patricia. For the first time, she was hearing somebody, excluding her mother and daughter, speak in a positive manner toward her.

"What happened when you went to Wheeler County?"

"In 1985, when I was eighteen, Patricia, ah... Mrs. Wagger, her two children, and I went to visit her mother and daughter. I had known her for about two weeks when she invited me to go, and I accepted."

"Did you have a relationship with Mrs. Wagger before this?"

"Well, we were friends. I played with her children, and she and I talked, but we didn't have a sexual relationship."

"Once you got to Wheeler County, did you have a sexual relationship with her?"

"Yes, Sir."

"Where did that take place?"

"In the back bedroom of her mother's trailer!"

"After you returned from Wheeler County, did you continue your relationship with Mrs. Wagger?"

"No! She said she was going back to her husband and it was over."

Mr. Marks had no further questions. I wondered why none of these men were asked if Patricia had made any attempts to engage in unusual sexual activities, or suggested such to them. Wouldn't, I mean couldn't, that prove how insatiable she was?

Defense Attorney Roth began his cross-examination of this rebuttal witness.

"Mr. Vincent, how long had you known Mrs. Wagger and her children before you went to Wheeler County with them?"

"A couple of weeks."

"Did the kids seem to like you?"

"Well, they seemed to. We had a lot of fun together. They were great kids."

"Did you ever visit the Wagger home when Walter was there?"

"Yes, Sir."

"How well did Patricia and Walter get along while you were there?"

"Not very well! He yelled at her a lot. Slapped her in front of me! When I saw him slap her, I left. It was the following day when we went to Wheeler County."

As he left the courtroom, I was convinced he really did care for Patricia and her children. That brief affair in Wheeler County just might have been a Godsend. It was two weeks that Patricia had a true friend, and in that friend, she found love, even if for only a short time! During that time, she and the children experienced no beatings, no name-calling. She needed him, and he was there. She said she intended to stay with him, but good ole Walter came to the rescue, and good ole Patricia went home again.

David appeared honest and sincere. In his attempt to leave the stand, he gazed at Patricia. While his time in this courtroom was over, I had a gut feeling that someday I would come in contact with David Vincent one more time.

It was becoming monotonous, but neither side was willing to give in. Not one spectator wanted to give up either, just in case another Gertrude Solene was to appear. That was not likely. She was one of a kind!

Witnesses continued with Polly Billingston, Patricia's sister-in-law. Her testimony was quite brief.

"Did you ever visit the home of Walter and Patricia Wagger?"

"Once in awhile."

"Did you ever see Mrs. Wagger with a black eye or any bruises?"

"No."

"Ever know of any time Walter Wagger beat his wife?"

"No."

"Did Evelyn Billingston come to live with you after the shooting?"

"Yes."

"Did the two of you ever sit down and talk about the shooting?"

"Yes. She said she knew Patricia had asked Colin to shoot Walter, and she had asked her, too."

"Has Mrs. Billingston been to your house since Mrs. Wagger went to jail?"

"She stopped by on her way to Wheeler County, but she never got out of the truck."

"Have you talked with Mrs. Billingston since she moved back?"

"No."

A real close family, I thought. At a time when they should be pulling together, they were pushing farther apart. What was Mr. Roth going to do with this one? Even Patricia's family was denying having seen any signs of physical abuse. The key words seemed to be "seen" and "heard." Either the allegations had been fabricated, or the defendant had spoken to very few people about her home life. Maybe it all dealt with what waited for her when she got home if Walter heard or thought she had breathed a word.

"Mrs. Billingston, do you know Jeremy Brentwood?"

"Yes."

"How are you associated with him?"

"He is my brother-in-law, married to my sister."

"Were you and your husband, Michael, married when Mr. Brentwood went to prison?"

"Yes, we were."

I could see the puzzled look on many faces as we all wondered where in the hell this line of questioning was going.

The story of Jeremy Brentwood! The man who alleged that Patricia was responsible for his jail sentence; he claimed her testimony in his trial gave him time in prison for armed robbery.

Next in line was none other than Patricia's half-brother himself, Michael. He was the son of Patricia's father by his first marriage. What happened to his mother? No one ever said, no one ever asked.

"Mr. Billingston, did you ever visit the home of Patricia and Walter Wagger?"

"Not too often."

"Did you ever see Walter abuse his wife?"

"Nope!"

"Ever see her with a black eye or bruises?"

"Nope!"

"Did she ever tell you that Walter hit her?"

171

"Nope!"

That was it! The prosecution was finished with this witness almost as soon as he was sworn in. Michael and Polly were common folk: Michael, somewhat overweight and in dire need of a shave, Polly unfashionably dressed with basically no hairstyle and no make-up. They all seemed to follow the same pattern having only what they needed.

Defense Attorney Roth was not going to let this one go just yet.

"Mr. Billingston, do you know Jeremy Brentwood?"

"Yep!"

"Did you ever testify in his favor during a trial?"

"Yep!"

"Wasn't that because of an incident which occurred between you and Patricia, at which time you ended up in jail?"

"Nope!"

"Didn't you say, during that trial, that you didn't think Patricia was very truthful?"

"Yep, that is what I said."

"Didn't you say that because she once testified against you, and you spent sometime in jail?"

"Yep!"

"Isn't that why you came here today? To testify against your sister because she once testified against you?"

"Nope!"

"Aren't you just trying to get even with her?"

"No!"

That was the first time Michael's voice had changed. He went from "nope" to "no." It was my opinion this hostility began a long time ago, and it was a get-even situation. Payback time!

It was beginning to get a little easier to understand why Patricia had put up with the abuse. Even her family, with the exception of her mother, either hated her or resented her for one reason or another. She couldn't feel love, except motherly love, because that's all she had ever felt.

Her testimony and the testimony of Megan gave justification to ending the pain. The manner in which it was done was still out in left field.

Patricia had no friends and seldom visited with her family. Maybe that was Walter's intention — out of sight, out of mind!

CHAPTER 34

The next witness would take us back to Patricia's testimony concerning the IUD. I did not need to search back through my notes to recall her allegations. It was still a very clear recollection — she had stated that Walter removed the IUD himself.

Prosecutor Smith asked Dr. R.I. Hickman to explain the IUD, or intrauterine device.

Dr. Hickman was pleasant looking in an odd sort of way. He was tall and thin, with a touch of gray in his hair that made him look quite distinguished. He spoke softly in a tender way. I could understand how he could make any woman feel comfortable during an examination and in seeking birth control.

The general practitioner from St. Jacob's Hospital began.

"The IUD acts as a foreign body in the womb which prevents the egg from implanting. The device is inserted through the vagina, into the mouth of the womb, and pushed into place. The string is cut, usually leaving an inch or less hanging down. The device is removed with a speculum by opening the vagina and using forceps to pull on the string."

"Can you tell us what the size of the opening of the vagina is?"

"After a woman has had children, it is generally less than a quarter inch."

"The defendant testified earlier in this case that her husband reached up inside her and removed the IUD with his hands. Do you believe that to be true?"

"It would be highly impossible! I am not saying it cannot be done, but assuming a woman is normal, you would have to use two fingers and a thumb to grasp the string. Most women who wear the IUD can barely find the string themselves."

During the time of his testimony, Dr. Hickman displayed a model of the vagina and the IUD. He was the expert! He found it highly unlikely, but I doubt the scene with the dog was anything of which a normal person would be a part. I was somewhat devastated that this doctor was so adamant about his conclusion this was all but impossible. How could anyone dream up such a well-defined incident that, medically speaking, was impossible to occur? Was Patricia so clever that, while locked up in her jail cell, she was able to concoct such a vivid story just to gain sympathy from the jury? The fact that any one human being possessed the gift to be so conniving was more than I could comprehend! However, stranger things had happened, and had been told right here in this courtroom!

I anticipated the turning point in this case. Would it arrive now that one of the major incidents of abuse had been described as "highly impossible?"

Defense Attorney Roth wasted little time.

"Dr. Hickman, are the vaginal openings of women who have given birth larger than those of women who have not?"

"That is correct!"

"If a man used an extension during love-making, would that cause the opening to be larger?"

"Are you speaking of a penile extension?"

"Yes, Sir."

"Then yes, a penile extension would cause this."

"Is it possible for an IUD to move down?"

"If that occurred, then the human hand could remove the IUD from the vagina."

"If the human hand did remove the device, would it cause much pain or any bleeding?"

"I would imagine such an occurrence to be very painful. Anytime the device is removed, there is some bleeding involved."

Prosecutor Marks asked one last question: "Is it possible for a woman to expel this device without knowing she has done so?"

"It's possible, especially during the menstrual cycle."

From Dr. Hickman's description of the removal, Patricia had her facts straight. How could she possibly have known this if it had not taken place? Dr. Hickman felt it highly impossible given half the facts, but given all the facts, it was certainly possible. It was difficult to imagine, but it was just another inexplicable event in the continuing saga of the life of Patricia and Walter Wagger. That life still remained a mystery to me!

CHAPTER 35

We were approaching the last of the rebuttal witnesses. I was anxious to see the grand finale. I was also anxious to get back to my normal, yet quite boring, life!

Finally, the infamous Jeremy Brentwood, in person! I had already formed my picturesque opinion of him, and he did not disappoint me. He was scruffy, with poor hygiene, yet dressed for the occasion — polyester suit and tie, left over from the seventies. Wearing a white shirt and unpolished shoes, he took his place to face the defendant one last time.

"Mr. Brentwood, are you currently serving a prison sentence?"

"No. I was recently released on a full pardon from the governor."

"What were you serving the sentence for?"

"I was sentenced in March 1982, to seven years for armed robbery."

"When did the robbery occur?"

"In August 1981."

"When did you meet Patricia Wagger?"

"I don't know. I guess I met her in April 1981."

"How did you meet her?"

"I am good friends with her brother, Michael. I was at his house one night when she came up, and we were introduced."

"Was she married to Walter Wagger at the time?"

"Yes, but I guess they weren't getting along or something."

"Did you have an affair with Mrs. Wagger during the time she was married to Walter?"

Please God, no!

"Yes! He was living somewhere else. We would go over to her mother's house after she had gone to bed. We'd spend the night together, then I'd get up and leave before her mother got up."

It must have been a quiet affair! He snuck in, they had sex, and he snuck out, never disturbing her mother! Hmm, no witnesses to this affair either!

"Did you know Walter Wagger?"

"I didn't really know him. I had met him once or twice."

"Did you ever see Mrs. Wagger or her daughter, Megan, with bruises on them?"

"Yes, many times!"

"Do you know where they got those bruises?"

"One night, she told me Walter had been beating on her and the girl."

"Was there ever a time when Mrs. Wagger asked you to kill her husband?"

"Yes! One night in bed, she told me she was fed up with Walter beating on her all the time. She told me if I would kill him, she would marry me. Hell, I didn't want to marry her to start with, and I told her I wasn't gonna kill no one. So I got up and left!"

There we had it! The gospel according to Jeremy! In the heat of passion, during an affair that had been going on for sometime, she interrupted the mood to ask him to kill her husband, a husband who had been living somewhere else! But the request was not without rewards! She offered to marry him, and from the looks of Jeremy, he was not going to get too many offers.

Prosecutor Smith refrained from any further questions, but Defense Attorney Roth welcomed the opportunity to take over.

"Mr. Brentwood, would you say you've been a good boy while you were in prison?"

"No!"

"Have you any idea why you were pardoned?"

"Hell, no! It came as a total shock to me."

"Did you commit any unlawful offenses while you were in prison?"

"I guess twelve or thirteen."

"I believe the number of offenses is fourteen."

"If you say so!"

"It's not what I say; it's what the court papers say."

"Well, I suppose they should know."

"I believe the last one occurred in August 1987."

"If that's what it says."

"When did you leave the state prison?"

"In October 1987."

"And you have no idea why you were pardoned?"

"I said I didn't."

Jeremy was beginning to become defensive, and Mr. Roth knew he had pushed his buttons. Did he know why Mr. Brentwood had been pardoned? If he did, he kept it a secret and asked no further questions.

As Mr. Brentwood left the witness stand, he looked in the direction of the defendant — a face he never saw! Patricia kept her head down — from being ashamed or disappointed, who could tell?

Patricia had testified against him in a court of law. A testimony that, according to Jeremy, had cost him five years of his life! He had revealed something to her in a moment of passion, telling her how he had robbed a grocery story and held the clerk at gunpoint until he was given all the money she had. Patricia had been sworn under oath to tell the truth. Unfortunately, for Jeremy, that truth was against him.

In a moment of passion, Patricia had asked him to kill her husband. He said no. He swore under oath to tell the truth. Had he?

Today, Jeremy appeared in this court and returned the favor.

Did she testify against him because he would not kill her husband? Did he testify against her because she sent him to jail? He was free now, thanks to the governor's pardon. Patricia's taste of prison still lay in wait.

Oh, the sweet taste of revenge!

CHAPTER 36

The courtroom was quiet, the hallway busy, hundreds of people standing in view of the door, waiting for the opportunity to catch a glimpse of the happenings inside! There was no room, and there had not been an empty seat from day one. It was amazing to see this many people housed in one place without someone giving away freebies. Many refused to take a lunch break or leave the courtroom during recess. Most arrived in the morning hours at least an hour before court was to begin. This trial was non-denominational! Children, parents, grandparents — all had sat through the many hours of tiresome, redundant, and often emotional testimony. Everyone seemed to want to hear the facts surrounding the fiction that had circulated along the streets and rural areas for more than a year. Some of them were hooked now! I had to wonder how many of these facts had truly changed their opinion.

The last known residence of the Waggers before they moved to the Harald Apartments was a small farmhouse owned by Doy Alfred in unincorporated Farmtown. Mr. Alfred finally gave Walter an eviction notice when the rent was well over three months past due. He was on the stand ready to testify about the day he approached Walter with the notice.

"Mr. Wagger told me that he was sorry he hadn't paid the rent but that his wife had left him, and he just wasn't thinking straight. He stated that Patricia had always taken care of the bills, and he didn't know where everything was. He said he would have the money to me in the next hour or so, but he never brought it to me. The next thing I knew, they had moved."

Was it still her fault the bills had not been paid? It was Walter who promised to bring the money but chose to hide in the bushes and move instead.

Mr. Alfred further stated that he had heard the Waggers argue a lot but added, "I never saw her with any bruises on her. I did see some on the little boy, but I don't know where they came from."

"Mr. Alfred, did you ever see either Mr. or Mrs. Wagger abuse their children?"

"Not really abuse them. One day I was driving by the house and stopped by to talk to Mr. Wagger about the rent. The little boy was in the yard fighting with his sister, who was visiting, over the last dip of snuff. The mother took the snuff from the little boy and told him the girl should have it. The little boy and girl finally split the dip. I never saw her hit him or anything. He just started crying after she took it."

Defense Attorney Roth asked Mr. Alfred if he ever spoke with Patricia concerning the rent being due or anything about the house.

"No. Anytime I went to the house, Mr. Wagger always met me in the yard."

"So you really don't know much about Mrs. Wagger and the children?"

"No, Sir! Only what Mr. Wagger told me the day he said she left."

CHAPTER 37

The trial was now becoming mostly hearsay. Through the entire trial, no one really knew this family. The only real proof came from those within the home. Gertrude and her husband had engaged in sexual activities with Patricia and Walter, but according to Gertrude, it was consensual. No one really witnessed the abuse, only evidence that it had occurred. Most of those who had seen the bruises, black eyes, and busted lip testified to having no idea how they had gotten there. She never said, they never asked!

Prosecutor Marks asked and was granted a ten-minute recess.

"Your Honor, our last witness is Sheriff Gossett. This could be a lengthy testimony. I'd like to suggest the court be allowed to take a ten-minute recess so we can start fresh with no interruptions."

"Very well, Mr. Marks. This court stands in recess."

It was fascinating to watch the many faces turn one to another and remark, "Did he say last?"

I had to admit that phrase was music to my ears. Even the defendant looked relieved! She stood up and looked around for a hint of support. When she looked in my direction, it was brief, almost non-existent. I would have given her that smile of that support, but there wasn't time. Her eyes were swollen, maybe from crying, maybe from lack of sleep. As for what she was feeling, it was anybody's guess!

During most of the trial, with the exception of her testimony, her back was toward us. When she entered and exited the courtroom, she seldom looked in our direction. She walked with her head down, the portrait of a whipped puppy.

Had she been beaten? No doubt! But I had been wishing the same thing I knew she was: Had she only pulled the trigger herself!

During her testimony, we saw each of her identities: a shattered and abused woman, a woman who had loved and lost, a mother and a wife, and a woman who had been introduced to hatred by the same man who had introduced her to love!

She had smiled when she spoke of good times! She cried when she spoke of the bad! Most of the emotion we saw was that of sadness. She was human, capable of emotions, but on February 27, 1987, she became numb. She could no longer cry or even hate. He could hurt her no more! When she stopped hurting, all those emotions turned to anger, and the urgency to end it all overpowered her.

Patricia could not remember how she felt at the time of the shooting, or what she was thinking when it occurred! In her own words, she was not feeling and she was not thinking. It apparently had hit her when she heard the doctor say, "Your husband died on the operating table."

Once again, those emotions came back!

Maybe this last time she could have left! Maybe she could have made him love her more! Maybe this time he would have kept his promise to make it stop! But this time, it was too late!

Twenty-four hours before the shooting, she had a choice. But as the midnight hour came to a close on that dreadful night, she let go of that choice.

Had the killing of her husband accomplished a thing? It was true the physical, verbal, emotional, and sexual abuse was gone, but so were her mother, her children, and her identity. I was sure that, in the past year, she had changed.

Even the psychiatrist had said that in the June evaluation, just before the trial began, she was no longer suffering from low self-esteem. I was sure she could now see the situation more clearly and could have done things differently! But would she?

It was too late! She had become hard-hearted! No man was ever going to hurt her again! I knew that deep in the pit of her soul lay the one obstacle that had put her in this masquerade. He had kept her there for as long as she had stayed, and that same obstacle helped her find her way out. Deep inside her was that emotion she could not run from. Deep down in her inner being was love.

Patricia had been abused for so long! Walter brought her back with the promise of love. "I will never do it again!" That night something happened! She lost that love! Maybe she had lost her love for Walter, but the love for her mother, her children, and her life was foremost in her mind.

181

She wanted a way out. By midnight, she saw no other way. She knew — right or wrong, she could not take this walk alone. Alone, there was no way out.

Through Megan she found that strength!

CHAPTER 38

It was the longest ten minutes I had spent in the courtroom, my mind working overtime as I tried to imagine nine years worth of torture that ended in one split second. I had not taken the time to dwell on the outcome, just what had occurred day by day. Until the prosecution mentioned "last witness," it didn't really dawn on me what Patricia and the children had to anticipate.

If this jury convicted her, she would in some way be in the same situation as before. There would be no one to love her! She would be without her children, and from this, she could not go back to be with them. It would be years before she saw sunlight outside the prison grounds, years before she slept in a bed built for two. The world would keep turning, but outside those prison walls, she would not know it.

If she was acquitted, she could get on with her life! What life? She had lost her children, who were now living in separate foster homes. Would the State ever find her fit enough to be a mother to them? Would she go back to her friends at the Harald Apartments? Would she go back to her life on welfare? What were her choices?

Regardless of my feelings toward her, somehow and in someway, somebody had to pay for this murder. Was it enough for Patricia and Megan to live with this for the rest of their lives and apart from each other? I didn't think so!

Nobody wanted this child to carry the burden alone. Nobody wanted to send this woman to prison. Yet everybody wanted to see the one responsible punished for the crime.

Even Patricia knew she was responsible!

Walter had taken every opportunity to prove he was the boss. This family would do whatever Walter deemed necessary, or the consequences would be extreme. He called it maintaining control, keeping his children from going wild! But nobody ever pleased Walter.

Still, he was a human being, even though I used the term loosely! A man shot down in the prime of his life. He had hurt so many people, and he justified it all. It was all about Walter! What Walter wanted!

It should have been vengeance of the law, but when she called, nobody responded. When others called, nobody came. Nobody saw, and nobody heard.

What if he had awakened before Megan shot him? What if he had meant what he said about killing Patricia if she was not gone? What if, what if, what if?

The same pattern he had followed for three days would have more than likely been followed. He had not calmed down since his arrival! He might have killed someone. He might have apologized and promised not to do it again. He might have filed for divorce and followed through with it. He just might have woken up with thoughts of the jeep on his mind, or his wife having an affair, and Tuesday would have been a remake of the previous three days.

Megan's words kept reverberating in my ears: "He told Mom if she was still there when he got back, he was going to kill her. I knew somebody was going to die."

This was one time the alcohol was for the good! Passed out, Walter never knew or felt a thing. Every one knew somebody was going to die. Every one knew it was just a matter of time. That morning, somebody did!

I felt my blood flowing in a heated sort of way as Prosecutor Marks called his last witness to the stand. The reiteration of Sheriff Gossett's testimony was about to begin. I knew it was necessary to bring him back. The complexity of his first bout on the stand was more than this jury could possibly assimilate at one time. Besides, it was the prosecution's last chance to dispute Patricia's testimony.

For the past several days, I, along with spectators and members of the jury, had heard an enormous amount of evidence presented in this case. There was no doubt the shooting had taken place, and no doubt who had pulled the trigger! I knew why it happened. I knew Megan pulled the trigger. I knew Patricia had coerced Megan. I knew Walter was the victim. I also knew Walter had instigated the crime by having victimized his family for all those years!

On the final day of the trial, the defense had one last chance to prove reason for doing what she did – for what both of them did!

Prosecutor Marks began.

"Sheriff Gossett, did you ever engage in a conversation with Evelyn Billingston?"

"Yes. On April 19, 1987, I spoke with Mrs. Billingston at the Welfare Department in Wesburg."

"Why did you have that conversation with her?"

"I wanted to interview her pertaining to the incident which occurred on February 27, 1987. I conducted a question and answer type interview with her. Mrs. Billingston was seventy-six years old at the time. I began to ask her about the occurrences which led to the shooting. I first asked her if Patricia had talked to her about killing Walter. She said that Patricia had told her she tried to poison Walter by putting some poison in his coffee, but she must not have gotten enough. I then asked her if Patricia had asked her to shoot Walter. She said yes, that Patricia had asked her if she could shoot the gun to kill Walter. The next question was if she had ever heard Patricia ask Colin if he could shoot Walter. She replied yes, she had, but Colin said no."

At first, I wondered what more this Sheriff could possibly say, but by now, I realized this statement by Mrs. Billingston was making quite an impact. The attempt to prove premeditation had taken us back to the time Patricia had written a letter to her mother asking for rat poison. It had just become more prevalent this weekend. This was not the first time we had heard someone admit to hearing Patricia ask others to kill Walter.

Always before, when the fighting broke out, the urge to kill her husband surfaced. When Walter calmed down, the idea left her mind – until the next time! Why not this time?

The witness continued!

"I then asked Mrs. Billingston what started the fighting on the weekend before the shooting. She said a man from Florida had come to Appleton. Patricia was seeing him, and he wrecked the jeep. I asked her who had the kids when Patricia came to Wheeler County. She replied Walter had them."

Mrs. Billingston's statement to Sheriff Gossett was conflicting with that of Patricia and David Vincent, who both stated the children went with them. Mrs. Billingston herself had testified the kids came with them to visit. With so many inconsistent versions, I had to wonder if any of us would ever know what really happened.

"I proceeded by asking her where she was at the time of the shooting. She said she was in bed when she heard the shot. I asked her to tell me what she did after she heard the shot. She said she got up and went into the kitchen. She said, 'I heard Patricia calling the police.' She said Patricia told her, 'See Mommy, I told you it was going to happen.' I then asked Mrs. Billingston if Walter sent money home and she said yes, but just enough to pay some bills, but most of the time Patricia never paid them."

I noticed Prosecutor Marks looking quite pleased as he completed the questioning of Sheriff Gossett. The statement would prove to be quite damaging, even though it did not jive with the previous testimony of Mrs. Billingston.

Defense Attorney Roth was raring to go.

"How long did this interview last?"

"I guess about a half an hour."

"Did Mrs. Billingston tell you when Patricia said she was going to kill Walter?"

"She said about two months before the shooting."

"Did your department remove any other weapons from the Wagger home following the shooting?"

"Other than the murder weapon, we removed some knives."

"Did your deputies think those knives might be important since Patricia had told them about the incident with the knife?"

"Yes."

What, pray tell, was the purpose of these questions? The last chance the defense had and what was Mr. Roth accomplishing?

The prosecutor sat quietly in his chair for a moment, looking as if he was about to ask the question that would remove any doubt. The silence was broken when Mr. Marks declared, "Your Honor, the State rests!"

CHAPTER 39

All that stood between this case and the jury was the closing arguments. All that stood between Patricia and prison was the jury. All that stood between me and my normal life was the verdict!

I anticipated the closing arguments would be quite lengthy and powerful. The last thing heard is the first thing remembered!

Defense Attorney Ray took this opportunity to make the motion that the jury be instructed to return a verdict of not greater than manslaughter.

Judge Kimble quickly denied the motion.

Judge Kimble began to address the jury: "Ladies and gentlemen of the jury, I remind you to determine the facts in this case and apply the law to the evidence presented and the evidence alone. Your verdict must be returned beyond any reasonable doubt. Your choices in verdicts: (1) murder in the first degree; (2) murder in the second degree; (3) voluntary manslaughter; (4) involuntary manslaughter; (5) not guilty."

There was no choice of "guilty by responsibility." This choice could not be an easy one!

Prosecutor Marks began his closing argument in the same fashion that he had begun the opening one.

"Ladies and gentlemen of the jury, you have sat through several days of testimony. By now, many of you are tired and would like to go home to see your families. Some of you may already have made a decision as to which verdict you should return. The question at hand is whether or not Megan Billingston was acting on behalf of her mother when she shot and killed Walter Wagger. I'm going to take you back to what happened when Walter Wagger arrived home on February 24, 1987. He came home after being gone for two weeks and found a mess. Who caused the argument that ensued? When he came home the last time, he said to his wife, 'Bitch, I thought I told you to be gone.' Then he sat down in the chair and passed out.

"During the course of the weekend, Patricia Wagger had asked her eleven-year-old daughter to kill Walter. Imagine, if you will, that while Walter is passed out in the chair, she thinks about what she should do. She has her daughter to get the gun and turn off the lights. Then, Megan goes to bed. Patricia then goes into the bedroom and gets Megan up for the sole purpose of killing her husband. As her daughter prepares to shoot Walter, Mrs. Wagger stands in the kitchen with her hands over her ears. It takes her daughter three tries! After Mrs. Wagger takes care of the gun, she sends her daughter back into the living room three times, and on the third try, the gun fires. The bullet hit Walter Wagger just below the chest.

"Mrs. Wagger had three opportunities to stop the shooting, but she didn't do it. Then she told the police — and had her daughter to tell the same story — that she was asleep when the shooting took place. Was it done intentionally? Yes! There was malice involved! It was premeditated! She had talked with her daughter for two days about it. She had gotten the gun down and loaded it the day before. When someone uses an innocent person to commit murder, he or she is responsible for that murder.

"In order for this to have been self-defense, the law states that a person must feel they are in eminent danger. This was not the case! Walter Wagger had been drinking since the early morning hours. He passed out in the chair. Why didn't she leave? She stated she couldn't even get him awake to eat. So why didn't she just leave?

"Ladies and gentlemen, you have to decide who is telling the truth. You are the sole judges. The State asks that you return a verdict of murder in the first degree."

As Prosecutor Marks returned to his seat, I thought about all he had said. Well, all that I could remember. Over and over, he had asked the same question: why didn't she leave? Not only this time, but all the times before! In her testimony, she defended that action, giving many reasons for the actions and for those times when she didn't take any action. From loving him to hating him, why she stayed to why she finally had him shot! Her reasons were justified, but the manner in which she carried it out was not!

Patricia never denied being responsible for the death of her husband. She was frightened. She was sore. Finally, she just became numb! She stated if she got the chance, she was going to kill him, but, in the end, she passed down that chance to her daughter.

Defense Attorney Ray, looking less confident than he had in the opening statements, was rustling through his notes, making sure he did not leave out one shred of evidence in his closing arguments.

I kept my eyes glued to Patricia in an effort to see her reaction. She had none!

"Ladies and gentlemen of the jury, we have proven that Walter Wagger was a violent man. We do not, and will not, consider Megan responsible for this murder.

"You heard Patricia say there were times when Walter was a kind man, but it wasn't very often. Consider the children! The incident with the knife and the impact that incident left on this family.

"Mr. Marks would have you believe that the injuries Patricia sustained during the weekend before the shooting were minimal. Megan, Patricia, and Mrs. Billingston all testified to witnessing Walter Wagger as he struck his wife several times during those three days. Try and remember what that weekend was like: the defendant had not bathed, had not changed her clothes, had not prepared a meal, and had not slept. How would you respond if someone spat in your face or threatened your life? You heard testimony that Walter Wagger, when he filed for divorce, wanted Megan. The truth is, he not only didn't want her, he didn't even like her.

"Ladies and gentlemen, Patricia Wagger didn't want her husband dead, she just wanted the pain to stop.
At the time of the shooting, she was a desperate woman. Megan was in fear! Patricia was in fear! Neither of them is to blame for the crime that was committed.

"This trial is about the right to protect yourself and your family. The right to feel free and to be free in your own home! Patricia and her children did not have that freedom when Walter was home. The person who put that fear in that home is the person who killed Walter Wagger — he killed himself!

"He taught his family to live in fear whenever he was home. When you live in fear, you learn fear! The ones who wanted to love him, he taught them to hate him! In spite of everything, Patricia did love Walter. God knows why, but she did! Walter had taught Megan to hate him. She had no love for him at all. Walter taught his family the way to solve your problems is through violence.

"What were her options? She had called law enforcement, but nobody came! She had left, but each time he called her a tramp and tracked her down. For many reasons, she always came back. Consider the marriage, the abuse, the weekend! Consider who is really to blame! Is it really the one who was protecting her family and their freedom? We ask that you weigh the evidence presented in this case and bring back a verdict of not guilty."

Attorney Ray presented quite a case in his closing argument, but was it too late? Patricia Wagger was guilty, but guilty of what? Even after all the testimony we had heard, nobody really knew what happened except the two involved! The talking was over. The jury had heard all they were going to hear. The decision was up to them.

The case of the State of West Virginia versus Patricia Jane Wagger had now come to a close.

As Judge Kimble instructed the jury to retire to the jury room, I was unable to look at her. For the first time, I did not want to see her eyes. I looked for Megan but could not find her. All I wanted to do now was leave this courtroom, write my story, and never look back. All of a sudden, I didn't want to know the verdict. It was difficult! Knowing what was right by law, to separate the reason for the murder from the way it was done. Where had this obsession begun for me? Worse yet, where was it going to end?

The facts were all in! For nine years, she had loved this man. For nine years, she had lived in fear. For nine years, she had taken this abuse.

According to testimony, for nine years, she had dreamed of a way to end it. She had asked her mother, her son, and her lover to help her get out. She only knew one way to put an end to this, so then she asked her daughter — the one person who would do anything she asked. Even if it meant killing for her! Now, with all this behind her and with all she stood to lose, I had to ask, Was it worth it?

CHAPTER 40

I tried to place myself inside that jury room, allowing myself to think like one of the twelve! They were behind closed doors and had to agree on a verdict beyond any reasonable doubt. The five choices were complicated.

Did Patricia pull the trigger? The answer was no. Had the murder been premeditated? That was debatable, depending on whom you believed.

Patricia had undoubtedly spoken of killing Walter. She had apparently asked others to do it for her!
She, herself, had countless opportunities to kill him at a time when self-defense could have been a valid defense but she never acted on them.

It was tough! Just as she knew somebody was going to die, somebody had to pay for that death. Somebody had to pay for the abuse! Walter finally paid for the abuse. Who was going to pay for his death? The answer seemed logical, but is logic always what is fair?

Murder in the first degree, murder in the second degree, voluntary manslaughter, involuntary manslaughter, and not guilty! Premeditated was not an option. In reality, by law, she was guilty on all accounts. Choosing one was a hell of a decision to make! Maybe there should be a death-by-justified-reason verdict. That would make her guilty beyond a reasonable doubt!

The next six hours seemed like an eternity. I was hungry but unable to eat; tired, yet unable to rest; worried, and not sure why! It wasn't my freedom on the line, but often, I felt like this case was a big part of me. I had not been quite the same since the trial began. I had gotten a real education!

I understood the Battered Woman Syndrome — something, two weeks ago, I didn't even know existed!
I started out very angry with Patricia, pointing the finger and only knowing the

rumor about why we were going to trial: she had used her daughter to kill her husband. The life she was trying to escape was not mentioned! Once that situation was revealed, I had to ask what I would do in that situation. Why should anyone be forced to accept abuse as a way of life? It wasn't only the abuse that could be detected, such as physical and sexual, but also the verbal abuse that every one who came in contact with Walter suffered. But most important were the children. That verbal abuse over that weekend had put the entire family on an emotional roller coaster.

What gave him the right to call them names? What gave him the right to insinuate that she was an unfit mother? What gave him the right to give Megan the impression she was hated by all? He led her to believe she was the next best thing to garbage! Just because he married Patricia and sent money home to her, it did not make the abuse legal. He had a drinking problem, but did that make the abuse justified? He was a great guy to his friends, but did that make the abuse impossible to believe?

So many questions still remained, and the trial was over. They were questions that would never be answered.

Patricia stated that she stayed, and came back when she left, for the kids. They were all she had! Yet she allowed her firstborn to be raised by her parents because Walter didn't like her. Walter didn't want Megan. Everything was done to please Walter.

I understood the shooting. At last, she was fighting back! Mr. Roth was right when he said Patricia had lived in fear and violence for so long that it was all she knew. Walter had taught his wife and children well. Had that violence backfired on him? On that fateful day, his own teachings turned against him.

Patricia was an unpredictable woman. With the prosecutor, she was strong — she held her own. But she wasn't in fear of being beaten by him, nor had he threatened to kill her. The case presented by him might send her to prison, but how could that be worse than the abuse? In due time, she would be released from prison! With Walter alive, only death could release her from that hell to which she had grown accustomed.

She was sensitive, which brought about sympathy from anyone with a heart!

I was so wrapped up in my thoughts that I was startled when someone said, "The jury has reached a verdict."

The first words out of my mouth were, "I can't go!"

I had followed this trial, this family, this woman for so long, they had become a part of me! I could not bear the thought of seeing her when she heard the outcome. A friend of mine stood in the doorway with a look of exasperation.

He had been beside me everyday of this trial. To think, I was going to throw it away when the end was so near — that was more than he could comprehend!

"Are you crazy? You've got to go! You've come this far, don't let yourself down now."

I tried to make him understand that, for the past two weeks, I had spent every waking moment trying to sort this out. When I slept, I dreamed about them. I worried about their future. Where would they go? What was going to happen to them once that verdict was read? After two weeks of waiting for a solution now, in the sixth hour of deliberation, a jury of seven women and five men had reached a verdict. The truth was, I wasn't sure I wanted to hear their decision.

"You think she is innocent?"

"I don't know what I think! I'm only certain Walter Wagger was guilty. There is this fine line between innocent and murder. I just don't know where one crosses that line. I know she is responsible, but is that worthy of life in prison? You go ahead, and I'll meet you there."

"Do yourself a favor and follow this to the very end. You will live to regret it if you don't."

He was right, but I was not going to tell him so. I had no control in the verdict, but I owed it to myself to do as they did and fight to the bitter end. Maybe then, once and for all, I could put it behind me. Years later, it was obvious that I never would!

I wasn't there when the shooting took place, but often, I felt I had been. I knew what was in my heart. I knew the law. It wasn't for me to judge, nor was it for me to prove. As far as this court was concerned, I didn't exist. I had no control, not even of my heart, which felt an aching that would not go away. The defendant, Megan, the three Wagger children, and Mrs. Billingston! Even the one this court considered the victim! All impacted my life in some way.

I managed to pull myself together and headed for the courtroom. As I walked in, there he stood — my friend, camera in place, a smile on his face, waiting for the grand finale!

Any minute now, she would return to her seat one last time. One way or another, her trial was almost over. I was praying for the best, but I wasn't sure what that was. I realized it might be the worst. This decision was going to be man-made. I will never forget the look on her face when she appeared in that courtroom. Her expression was one of hope crossed with defeat. She barely looked up as she took her place again between her attorneys. The prosecution soon followed.

193

"All rise!" The judge and circuit clerk entered, Judge Kimble looking no more rested than he did when he left! He turned his attention to the bailiff, asking him to bring in the jury.

By now, I was numb. I suddenly knew that feeling she kept talking about, not feeling at all!

The jury returned to the batter's box one last time!

Judge Kimble took control.

"Let the record show all members of the jury are present. Members of the jury, have you reached a verdict?"

"Yes, Your Honor, we have!"

"Please hand your decision to the bailiff. Would you pass that to Mrs. Martin?"

The bailiff took the paper from the foreman's hand and handed it to the Circuit Clerk.

I began to shake as she began to read!

"We, the jury, find the defendant, Patricia Jane Wagger, guilty of murder in the first degree with the recommendation of mercy. So say all twelve of you ladies and gentlemen?"

All twelve voices resounded: "We do!"

The courtroom was silent! With the exception of the one person who whispered she knew it all along, the silence was deafening.

Patricia looked at Megan, who was seated directly behind her, to the right.

Megan faced her mother as tears ran down her cheeks. The next time the two of them would be this close, their bodies would be separated by bars.

I did not know what they were feeling, but basing it on my feelings, it was a terrible loneliness with a sigh of relief. My imagination was not vivid enough to put myself in the same situation!

Patricia smiled at Megan as if to say, "It's over!" She moved her lips and silently spoke: "I love you!"

At that moment, she turned to focus her attention on the judge.

Judge Kimble began what would be the last of the words he would speak for this trial: "Mrs. Wagger, this court has found you guilty of murder in the first degree! Have you anything to say?"

"No, Your Honor."

"Mrs. Wagger, the recommendation of mercy has been handed down along with your verdict. This means you will be eligible for parole after serving ten years. Post trial motions have been set for July 15, 1988. You have sixty days to appeal this verdict. You will remain in the custody of the Upland County

Sheriff's Department until post trial motions have been heard and sentencing has been handed down. This court stands adjourned!"

Although I wanted to slither out the back door and avoid the crowd, I had no choice but to remain seated until she had been removed. I became nauseated as the bailiff placed her in handcuffs and escorted her from the courtroom.

I watched Megan. She stood with her arms around Brother Claude. No matter what we all knew was the law, I somehow felt they never thought it would end with the maximum sentence. So many verdicts, but only one answer!

Why had I become involved? The life and times of the Wagger family left me in emotional turmoil. More importantly, it forced me to ignore that silent vow of remaining unbiased. No one ever warned me I would face such an ordeal!

Who in the hell were they anyway? For more then two weeks, they had disrupted my life, and for what? There was nothing I could do to help them! Nothing I could say to ease the pain. Nothing about me was going to make a difference in their lives. I was angry! But it wasn't at them.

They had lived through the most traumatic time. The keyword being "lived." In the end, life was all they had. Separate lives and miles apart!

I wanted to speak with members of the jury to find the basis of their verdict. But no one wanted to talk. The only issue seemed to be that she forced her daughter to pull the trigger. In their minds, Patricia had finally found someone to coax into committing a crime she had long been trying to execute. She felt there would be no punishment for a child, and once Walter was dead, it would all be over.

It didn't go that way! If she did indeed have a plan, then her plan fell through.

I wanted to go to her jail cell and speak with her, but what was I going to say? "Gee, I'm sorry you're here." Or maybe ask, "Did you really think you could get by with it?" Neither seemed appropriate!

I wanted to be a friend to her and Megan, maybe offer some assistance in getting them together more often. But they didn't even know me! Yes, they were lodged in my mind, but in their minds, I did not exist.

I kept thinking that maybe someday I could give them back a little piece of what they had lost. Although a large part of me wanted to leave this alone, something deep within told me I would never let go!

I found myself standing, waiting outside the courthouse for one last glance at Megan. She continued to show strength, knowing this nightmare was over, yet bearing in mind that today was the beginning of what was left of her childhood, alone! For nine years, Walter had kept her from her mother. In her eleventh year, he finally consented to letting them be together, not just for visits, but all the time! For Megan, at the age of eleven, the constant abuse began. She was seeing and hearing what her mother had spoken of often. In the short time she lived with them, what she was being exposed to became too much.

Patricia had lived with the abuse for nine years! As the relationship progressed, the abuse became worse. They had two weeks of freedom — two weeks without being beaten, spat on, screamed at, and accused — two weeks without fear!

Walter came home, and in three nights, he made up for the time he had lost.

This family had gotten a taste of the good life! Life without Walter!

Nine years, and three children later, Patricia had finally felt and tasted what life without abuse was like.

At the age of eleven, Megan carried out the threats she made about Walter to her school friends. At the age of eleven, Megan brought it all to an end!

I often wondered, did Patricia force Megan to shoot Walter, or just give her permission?

Patricia Jane Wagger was found guilty of first degree murder with the recommendation of mercy on June 22, 1988. On July 16, 1988, she was sentenced to life in prison with the possibility of parole after serving ten years.

Megan and the other three children, Colin, Michelle, and Michael, were placed in the custody of the West Virginia Department of Human Services in foster care. The youngest three remained together.

No appeal was ever made!

CHAPTER 41

In March 1990, almost two years after the trial of Patricia Jane Wagger concluded, I began my search for Patricia.

During those two years, I had kept tabs on the Wagger children.

Megan had been placed in a foster home in a nearby county. Colin, Michelle, and Michael were all still together in the foster home in which they had been placed after the shooting occurred. All were reported to be adjusting well. It was as if they had been saved in the knick of time! These children were proof that people do not have to grow up as products of their environment.

Day after day, I thought of Megan with a smile! Her strength and her vitality! I knew there was nothing and no one that was going to hold her down. Whatever her dream in life, there would be no road too long, no mountain too high, and no river to deep to stand in her way. She went to the greatest length to save her family. She would not stop for herself! Maybe her actions had separated them, but as she told her mother after the shooting, "There, Mommy, he won't ever hurt us anymore."

By the end of March, I had located Patricia in a correctional facility, miles away from Upland County! I sent her a letter asking her permission to put my views, my thoughts, and her story on paper. At first, she was reluctant, wanting to protect her children. We reached an agreement to change all names in an effort to keep the children from ever being exposed. Although many would remember, they would never have to relive it!

During our correspondence, she informed me she would once again be appearing in the Upland County courtroom, only this time in juvenile court. The social worker from the Child Protective Services, had filed a petition with the court asking that custody of the Wagger children be permanently awarded to the State. Once that was over, she would give her full consent to the story.

CHAPTER 42

On August 5, 1988, a month after Patricia Wagger was sentenced to life in prison, a petition was filed in Upland County by the Department of Human Services. The petition had been filed on the grounds of neglect and was requesting that permanent custody of the Wagger children be awarded to the Department.

On May 24, 1990, the case went before the Honorable Judge Kimble. Portions of the petition reverted back to the trial, such as the night Patricia ran down the balcony wearing no clothes; the fact she had coerced Megan to shoot Walter and permitted Megan and Colin to appear before the television cameras with Megan admitting to the murder; Patricia's previous requests that Colin shoot his father.

The petition further stated that Patricia had offered to relinquish custody of Michelle, who was then four years old, in exchange for bail money. The children's ages at the time the petition went to court: Megan, fourteen; Colin, eleven; Michelle, seven; and Michael, three.

Based on the fact that the Department felt the children had been abused and neglected by their mother, the Department asked the court to terminate Patricia's parental rights.

The children's hearing was closed, and the statements the children made were never revealed.

I walked into the courtroom just as the afternoon session was about to begin. Megan walked briskly through the courtroom carrying a vase with three red roses she had brought for her mother. It was close to Mother's Day!

The afternoon session did not last long. Patricia stated to me later that her lawyer, Attorney Carl Ray, had told her she didn't have a prayer. She consented to giving up her parental rights. She would later explain her decision to me: "Ten years is a long time. I can't take care of them. I can't see them when I want to! I can't tuck them in bed at night! I just can't offer them anything!"

She fought the battle on her own and won! She agreed to give up her parental rights, providing the children be permitted to spend major holidays with her. In addition, Megan could visit whenever she wanted! Her only other provision was that the children not be adopted without another hearing. Those conditions were granted!

During the original sentencing, Patricia was given visitation rights to see her children. It wasn't until she returned to Upland County for the petition hearing that she got to see Colin, Michelle, and Michael. Megan had been to the prisons to see her. This time, she was guaranteed visitation! She stated she would always be their mother but that, by the time she was able to take care of them, her children would be grown.

I once asked her who was the biggest influence in her life. She replied without hesitation, "My kids! They gave me purpose! They needed me and I needed them. Without them I was nothing! I'm trying real hard to better myself in this place, so that someday, when I get out, my kids can be proud of me."

What great lengths she had gone to better herself! Was it too late? Would those on the outside ever look beyond her faults to see her accomplishments? I hoped so!

CHAPTER 43

In April 1990, after much written communication, I saw her for the first time since the trial. The first time up close and personal!

At first glance, I knew she had changed! While we were only a month apart in age, she seemed so much older than I was. In a tank top and jeans, she was much different from the woman I had watched and listened to for two weeks almost two years before.

The tattoos on her arms were bold. The heart bearing Walter's name stood out far more than the others. She was kind, soft-spoken, and very polite. Her makeup somewhat tarnished her natural beauty. Her hair was frosted and much longer. There were no signs of abuse!

She seemed nervous, maybe a little excited!

We sat in a large visitation room. She served coffee from the community coffee pot, and we talked.

She talked very little about the trial or the incident. Patricia spoke mostly about her college classes and prison life itself! She was seeking desperately to find a new lawyer, one who would, at the very least, get some time shaved off her sentence. An early parole!

While prison life was far from glamorous, she spoke of trades she was learning and a life she had never known. She quit school at the age of sixteen and made only one attempt to return. She attempted to complete her GED, but Walter made her quit. Now, she had accomplished that and was studying psychology to further her education. The psychology would have helped in her younger days — maybe she would have known what made Walter click.

She was also working, her first real job with no fear of being forced to leave. We laughed — she was working for the West Virginia State Police! This time she was on the other side of the law.

Our first meeting was strained. I had a million questions but knew so little to say.

She felt the book was a good idea! I found she was still seeking approval. She had spoken with the prison warden and her best friend, Evonne Garrett, to get their opinion on the story. They both agreed the issue needed addressed. It was their approval I had actually been granted!

In many ways, she was still very childlike. She told me of one particular male inmate, Danny, who really liked her. "He always wants to sit by me at the movies. The other guys whoop and yell, "Danny likes Patricia! Danny likes Patricia." She laughed with a glow on her face. All that attention with no repercussions! I had to smile within. She then told me one story I shall never forget: a male inmate had been transferred here from an all male prison. When lunch time came, the others watched as he picked up the top slice of bread from his BLT. One inmate finally got the nerve to ask him why he was staring at the sandwich.

"I haven't seen bacon in so long, I just want to look it at for awhile."

The other inmates all began to laugh. She explained that "here" was one of the few prisons in the state that offered meat with the meals. It made me stop and realize all that I take for granted.

Megan and Patricia never discussed the shooting after the early morning hours of February 27, 1987. I guess they felt they had said all they needed to say.

When Patricia spoke of Megan, it was always with love. She had missed out on so much of her childhood. Megan was more like her baby sister than her daughter, they were so close in age! Because of the situation with Walter, Megan was raised by Patricia's parents. After her father died in 1981, Megan and Mrs. Billingston would come and stay with Patricia, sometimes two months at a time. Patricia and her mother agreed on one thing: "Because Walter hated Megan, it was best for her not to live with us. We always wanted to be together, but I guess now we will never have that chance. She always knew she was my daughter."

Then, when Walter moved his family into the house across from the Harald Apartments in 1986, Megan and Mrs. Billingston took up permanent residency with Patricia and her family.

The good ole Harald Apartments — the place to have affairs, party, beat your wife, fight with your neighbors, and lastly, where a child committed murder.

201

Nobody heard, nobody saw, nobody talked!

I wondered how much more these women would have to go through before the memory of their life with Walter was laid to rest.

My idea of prison life was far from tainted on my first visit. I had always pictured prison and airports to be the loneliest places in the world. As I sat there, I watched wives, husbands, and babies as they walked in to visit. Children sitting on Mommy or Daddy's lap, husbands and wives stealing a hug and a kiss! Tears were falling as parents tried to explain to the children why they could not go home that day!

It was difficult to bring myself to the realization that these people were here because each had committed a crime. They had been tried and found guilty of that crime. This was as close to staying on the inside of a prison I ever wanted to be.

CHAPTER 44

On the second visit, I asked her to tell me about prison life, beginning with her incarceration in the Upland County Jail.

"It was terrible! Boring and lonely! The first time being away from my children! I missed them so much! At night, I wanted to tuck them in bed, tell them goodnight and I loved them. But they weren't there! There were times when I didn't think I would make it through.

"From there, I went to Anderson, an all women prison. It was definitely different. A world inside a world! A city inside a fence! Population about fifteen hundred women, and all from different walks of life. We had a hall where we could go play pool and watch a big screen TV. We could go to the library, ride bicycles, or sit on a bench under a tree and just think about life. I did that a lot! There was still this loneliness, though, that no one could take away. At night, you'd lay awake, afraid someone would come in and cut your throat, because if you fell asleep, you couldn't get away. It's not a bad life, as long as you don't weaken!"

As far as the activities were concerned, it was more of a life than she had ever known.

"I spent six months at Anderson before being moved here to Prattville, a former school for boys. There are sixty women and one hundred and five men. Here we live and play by the rules. They seem to make up new rules as they go along. Since coming here, I have received my GED, several college credits, and numerous certifications for programs I have participated in. All in all, it's not as bad as I thought, though. I've accomplished more in here than I would have had the chance to do. It certainly has not been easy. But then again, nothing ever is."

As I listened to her talk, I realized how her life in prison was a lot like her life out of prison had been. She lived and played by Walter's rules. If she broke those rules, she suffered the consequences! After all, wasn't that how she ended up in here?

In each conversation about prison life, she couldn't seem to get past the loneliness — the sounds of hearing herself think, seeing the same faces everyday while none of them belonged to her family! She smiled a lot, but the bitterness remained.

She questioned why the deputies on duty did not heed to her calling, and why no pictures were taken of her bruises on the night of the shooting — questions her lawyers never asked during the trial.

"The jury who convicted me never saw what me and my kids went through that weekend. They never saw the abuse my eleven-year-old went through. What my nine- and six-year-old saw and felt. Not only that weekend, but every time Walter got mad."

Walter may have been out of her life, but the memories of her life with him would never go away. This was not a marriage, but a possession. Somewhere, the love she felt, enough to have an affair with a married man, was lost. Eventually, that love turned to hatred. I believed she had thought about getting out for a long time. I believed she had searched all possible routes. I believed she just ran out of time. The pain and anger became too much. At that point, when the fear of dying was in her mind, she did not do what she wanted to do, nor what she had to do – she did the one sure thing that would make it all go away. She created a scenario to end the pain! That scenario ended the life of Walter Wagger.

CHAPTER 45

In June 1990, almost two years to the date of the trial, a stranger walked into my office. He appeared with an employee of mine who introduced the young man as Skip. His face I could not place, but his voice was one I would never forget. I shook his hand as he stated, "It's a pleasure to meet you!"

There was no question in my mind as to where I had heard that voice before. His friend soon left the room, and the conversation between the two of us began.

"It's my understanding you have been in touch with Patricia."
Knowing what he meant, yet not knowing who his informant was, I hesitated to respond.

"I've been trying to get in touch with her, but no one seems to know where she is. I'm really David Vincent."

"Yes, I know who you are. What do you want from me?"

"I want a chance to talk to Patricia. I want her to know I still care, and that I haven't given up on her."

"So where have you been since the trial?"

"In Ohio! I wasn't sure she wanted to see me after all that has happened."

"So what makes you think she might want to see you now?"

He proceeded in telling me some intimate moments he had shared with Patricia during their two-week affair. A part of me believed he really did love her, or at least had never forgotten her! I told him I would not tell him anything but did consent to let Patricia know he had stopped by and wanted to speak with her. He had made quite an impression on me that day in the courtroom. If there was any shred of happiness to come out of all of this, I had no problem relaying the message. I lived up to my promise. The end result I've kept to myself. I

205

never saw him again.

I asked Patricia about her relationship with David, although I never revealed what he had already told me.

"I loved him! He was good with the kids! I wanted to be with him and stay when we left. I guess I just loved Walter more!"

Patricia and I never spoke of David again. I've often thought about him, wondered how his life might have changed had he and Patricia stayed together, if Walter had not once again made the idle promise to end the abuse, if David had returned to Patricia once the trial was over. Just another interesting twist to the "what ifs" in the life of Patricia Jane Wagger!

CHAPTER 46

It has been many years since the trial ended! A trial that changed the life of many, including myself!

Patricia served her time in prison, carrying her sentence of life with the recommendation of mercy to the final day! She was never granted an early parole.

Colin, Michelle, and Michael all remained in the same foster home. All three are grown and living lives of their own. They continued to have visitation with Patricia on major holidays and continue to maintain contact with their mother and Megan.

Megan has since graduated high school, attended college, and gotten married. While she no longer dwells on the shooting, at times the abuse that caused it doesn't seem to go away. She has overcome the fear and no longer judges people based upon the kind of man Walter was. She maintains the thought of that night: "Somebody was going to die." She now has her own life, but her mother, brothers, and sister still remain a very big part of that life.

Evelyn Billingston died in Riley General Hospital alone on February 19, 1991 — exactly ten years to the day of her husband, Martin's, death. She was eighty years old! She had been placed in a nursing home. There was no one to take care of her after Patricia was sent to prison. She became unable to take care of herself.

Patricia often spoke of the impact her parents had on her life.

"I felt so loved by them. Mom was forty-eight when I was born, and Daddy was fifty-one. I always felt so secure when they were near. Especially Daddy! Walter never abused Mom, me, or Megan when Daddy was around. Even though they are both gone, I still feel like they are watching over me and my kids. Growing up with them was good. I never had any brothers and sisters, and I was a spoiled brat. I was never that close to my half-brothers and sisters. I guess the biggest reason was the age difference. Mom or Daddy never abused or neglected me. That is why I knew they would take good care of Megan. When I became pregnant with Megan, Mom yelled a lot, but Daddy was just as calm as could be. He assured me that we would get through it. They raised Megan like she was their own. I didn't know when they took Mom to the hospital, so I never got to see her before she died. It hurts knowing her only child was locked up in a prison, just like it hurt every time Walter hit her or called her a bad name!"

Patricia has many regrets! She explains how now she can see things in a different light. That light takes her back to her very first experience of abuse from Walter. Had she only known the courage then that she has found today. Had she only stayed gone the first time she left.

It went on too long to even think about what to do!

The life of Walter Wagger really did make a difference! On February 27, 1987, the life of Walter Wagger came to an end! Twenty-nine years of age!

CHAPTER 47

So many times I think about the loss.

Nine years is a long time to spend with someone, only to have that person snatched away without warning. I do believe she loved him. I do believe he loved her. Patricia fought with him for nine years, leaving on occasion, but always coming back to stay. Walter abused her for nine years, but he always found her — couldn't live without her! He promised a whole new life if she would just come home! Where did it all go wrong?

In many ways, it was like a rebirth for all of them. The hell they went through all those years, the shame they endured once the deed was done, the humiliation suffered when their private life was exposed! Then, the learning to walk again after that life had ended! I was never there when the abuse took place, but I shall never forget the look in their eyes when they spoke of it.

Many people have said what they would do in a situation like this. I ask how anyone could know! How many of us could possibly fathom being forced to endure sexual abuse, physical abuse, and verbal abuse, not to mention what all that would do to your mental state! The prosecutor continued to say she could have left. Maybe she could have, maybe she should have. But she didn't.

Chapter 48

No one will ever know the entire story behind the early morning hours of February 27, 1987. We will never fully know or understand the conversations that took place between Patricia and her family. Many stories did not coincide! Who was right or who was wrong remains a mystery to me. But one can never dispute the abuse this family had suffered! We have all been placed in that situation where anger causes us to think and act in ways we normally would not — hurt that often pushes us over the edge. With no one to talk with about it, we stop thinking. We stop feeling! Maybe that is when we lose our conscience. No, we don't act out such vicious thoughts, but maybe we get over them soon enough. Knowing that feeling, try to tack on the physical abuse, the name-calling, and the threat of your life ending!

Somebody was going to die! All of them in that household were feeling that. Maybe there were other options, but none they had not already tried, many more than once!

Walter Wagger — a man who had proven to be a hardworking, good man! He never showed his demon to those who paid him; never showed his demon to his friends, unless he was drinking; never let his family reside in a place long enough to get help; never admitted he had a problem.

He always blamed his wife for his problems and inadequacies, always accused his wife of having an affair, always maintained control of his family at whatever cost!

Was he the victim?

Was Patricia looking for a way to get him out of her life once and for all? Not to end the pain, but to find her freedom?

Was Megan forced, coerced, or just given permission to do what she had told her friends she was going to do?

If Walter was the victim, it was only because the roles had been reversed!

If Patricia was looking for a way out, she found it! But for freedom, it was a high price to pay.

Megan used the opportunity to save her family from the monster they had all grown to hide from.

Walter's demon is buried, but its existence will never die.

Very few nights have gone by since the beginning of the trial that I have not thought about this family.

There's not a thought that does not include hurt for what Walter put them through, not a night when I don't think about the fear in which they lived. They never had to do a thing to bring on the abuse — it was their very existence that caused them pain.

Where are they now?

Separate homes, separate lives, but breathing! Not in fear! Not in pain! No more name-calling or constant fighting! Peace at last!

I'm not insinuating that I agree with the taking of a life, but I do believe that when Walter woke up, a life was going to be taken. God only knows where it would have ended! God only knows upon whom the wrath of Walter would have come down. I don't know where it was going, but I do know it came to an abrupt end. They no longer hear the verbal abuse, no longer feel the physical abuse! Patricia is free from the sexual abuse! I can't help but wonder if one ever gets past all the emotional damage/strain/pain/suffering/trauma, or do we just move on? Do we just survive?

My consolation came in knowing they all did survive. No matter where they are tonight, they are alive. I pray to God that they are – for who better than they deserve – "Sleeping Fearlessly."

Printed in the United States
24213LVS00004B/236